THE SURVIVAL IMPERATIVE

UPSHIFTING TO CONSCIOUS EVOLUTION

A Guide to Returning Peace and Harmony to the Planet

Also by

ERVIN LASZLO

Science and the Akashic Field (2006)

The Intelligence of the Cosmos (2017)

Reconnecting to the Source (2020)

The Immutable Laws of the Akashic Field (2021)

The Wisdom Principles (2021)

Dawn of an Era of Well-Being with Frederick Tsao (2021)

The Upshift Explorer with David Lorimer (2023, In Preparation)

Autobiography

My Journey (2021)

THE SURVIVAL IMPERATIVE

UPSHIFTING TO CONSCIOUS EVOLUTION

A Guide to Returning Peace and Harmony to the Planet

ERVIN LASZLO

author of *Science and the Akashic Field*

The information provided in this book is designed to provide helpful information on the subjects discussed. This book is not meant to be used, nor should it be used, to diagnose or treat any medical condition. The author and publisher are not responsible for any specific health needs that may require medical supervision and are not liable for any damages or negative consequences from any treatment, action, application, or preparation, to any person reading or following the information in this book.

References are provided for information purposes only and do not constitute endorsement of any websites or other sources. In the event you use any of the information in this book for yourself, the author and the publisher assume no responsibility for your actions.

Books may be purchased through booksellers or by contacting Sacred Stories Publishing.
Ervin Laszlo photo by Bernard F Stehle©

The Survival Imperative
Upshifting to Conscious Evolution
Ervin Laszlo

Print ISBN: 978-1-958921-17-3
EBook ISBN: 978-1-958921-18-0
Library of Congress Control Number: 2023931178

Published by Light on Light Press
An imprint of Sacred Stories Publishing, Fort Lauderdale, FL

Printed in the United States of America

ADVANCE COMMENTS BY INTERNATIONAL THOUGHT LEADERS

As a species, humanity has arrived at a crossroads. One road is to sleepwalk to extinction. The other road, which Ervin Laszlo shows so eloquently in this book, could help create a critical mass for a more peaceful, just, sustainable, healthier and joyful world. Only conscious evolution can save us.

—Deepak Chopra, MD, pioneer in integrative medicine, author of numerous *New York Times* bestsellers, including *Metahuman*

Indeed, it is only too true, as Ervin Laszlo writes, that we are reaching a tipping point. If we cannot get together to change the mindset of humanity, most importantly those in power, the decision makers, the influencers, we are doomed. And if we lose hope, we are doomed, for then why bother to take action? Our young people are faced with an enormous task as they grow into the planetary chaos we have created, and they need all the help and hope they can get. I hope this book will encourage and inspire people to pick up the baton and play a part in creating a 'brave new world' — before it is too late.

—Dr. Jane Goodall, DBE, Founder of the Jane Goodall Institute & UN Messenger of Peace

This is to be one of the most important and potent books of our time. All ages should read it as it offers rich and deep instructions on becoming the change that makes the change.

—Jean Houston, PhD, scholar, philosopher, author of over 30 books, including *The Possible Human*

This book catapults us beyond simply knowing that today's world is in the final throes of a dangerously unsustainable path. In seven concise chapters, scientist, philosopher and visionary Ervin Laszlo provides us a mind-map to the empowering new world that awaits us, as well as the thought-compass that guides us to that world with wisdom, love and grace. Long after we close the pages of *The Survival Imperative*, Ervin's words linger in our hearts as a compelling call to action that reveals our global, as well as personal, codes of transformation and healing.

—Gregg Braden, *New York Times* bestselling author of *The Divine Matrix* and *The Wisdom Codes*

Beyond climate change, social, political, and economic upheaval and religious and racial extremes, civilization is in a world of crises. Crisis ignites evolution! This chaos is a natural step in an unfolding process, rather than the tragic end to a broken planet. We are surrounded by evidence that we are on the threshold of a major evolutionary event, the dawn of *Conscious Evolution.*

The Survival Imperative, by the eminent science philosopher Ervin Laszlo, provides paradigm-shattering new knowledge that reveals the planet is experiencing an extraordinary evolutionary event … the dawn of a new civilization. Laszlo's bold and hopeful vision, defined as Conscious Evolution, provides new science to navigate this turbulent period in our planet's history, so that we may evolve from passive victims to responsible co-creators of the world to come.

Knowledge is power. The knowledge offered by Ervin Laszlo is truly the source of the *empowerment* needed to move beyond misperceived limitations and write new life-affirming stories for ourselves, our children, and the world. In the face of our current evolutionary upheaval, I personally believe that *The Survival Imperative* is a powerful prescriptive for helping civilization successfully evolve, or more accurately, thrive, into the future.

—Bruce H. Lipton, PhD, stem cell biologist and author of the bestselling books, *The Biology of Belief*, *Spontaneous Evolution* and *The Honeymoon Effect*

This book allowed me to understand Ervin Laszlo's belief that the Universe is conscious — and it also helped me to know what I could do, to feel a unique part of it, and to enjoy helping humanity and the planet progress positively.

—Andrew Lord Stone, Member House of Lords, UK Parliament

Vital information, if you care about your children's Tomorrow!

—Neale Donald Walsch, co-founder of Humanity's Team, author of the *Conversations with God* series

This invaluable book empowers the urgent potential for transformative action whose time has surely come. Founded on the emergent and unitive cosmology of our living Universe and planetary home, Ervin Laszlo extends a global call to embody its innate evolutionary impulse within our collective awareness, offering all of us and especially our young people an achievable vision and authentic hope for a world that thrives for the good of the whole.

—Dr. Jude Currivan, cosmologist, author and co-founder WholeWorld-View

A beautiful, inspiring and timely book, full of deep insights into humanity's present condition and the opportunity for change.

—Roger Casale, CEO, World Upshift Organisation

This indispensable and inspiring book, grounded in Laszlo's mastery of systems theory and the science of evolutionary consciousness, provides readers with a lucid, energizing, and visionary handbook for human survival at a historical moment of prevalent gloomy expectations. If its dire warning and hopeful planetary prescriptions are widely and urgently heeded, it could come to be interpreted as a liberation guide for the species on a global scale.

—Richard Falk, professor emeritus of international law, Princeton University, author of *This Endangered Planet*

Ervin Laszlo is a planetary sage, and in this succinct book, he distils the essence of a necessary blueprint for our future evolution based on a lifetime's study and encyclopaedic interdisciplinary knowledge. He lays out the essential principles and elements of a transformation of mindset and values, challenging us to come together to co-create a seismic systemic shift beyond our existing obsolete world views and values. A copy should be sent to every world leader and CEO of Fortune 500 companies, urging them to convene a well-publicised international conference on a genuinely human and regenerative future that transcends the agendas of the dominant oligarchy.

—David Lorimer, Programme Director, The Scientific and Medical Network (UK)

This extraordinary, extremely important new book by Ervin Laszlo explains clearly that if we continue to think and act as we did until now, we will endanger the future of our species. We are therefore called upon to make a great leap forward, to conscious evolution. The great merit of his book is to show us, on scientific grounds, how it is both necessary and possible for contemporary peoples and societies to achieve such a leap.

—Ignazio Masulli, former professor of Contemporary History, University of Bologna, author of *Nature and History: the Evolutionary Approach for Social Scientists*

A wake-up call that is so urgently needed by every leader and every human being — and then to be acted upon in oneness.

—Dr. and Master Zhi Gang Sha, author of *Tao Calligraphy*

A book of humanity awakening into conscious evolution. The development of civilization will never be the same any more.

—Frederick Tsao, 4th Generation Family Business Steward, author of *One Choice One World, The Rise of the Well-being & Happiness Economy*

Dr. Laszlo's book provides a powerful and fantastic blueprint on how we can create a new harmonious and loving society, with both ourselves and nature for many generations to come. We have advanced technology, but as Dr. Albert Einstein said, the creation of the atomic bomb and this technology changed everything except for humanity's thinking, and so Dr. Laszlo's book is an important step in changing our thinking for the better. Since the hardest part of a 1,000-mile journey is always the first step, Dr. Laszlo has given humanity that important first step in creating a beautiful, happy, and harmonious planet.

—Ted Mahr, Out of this World Radio, author of *Messages from the Masters* and *Journey to the Other Side: Talking to Angels and Other Benevolent Beings*

Immersed in the modern glory of growth, humanity has unfolded a new chapter in planetary history. Centuries of relentless passion and cravings notwithstanding, we have increasingly witnessed an abrupt, irreversible global crisis hurtling toward us. *The Survival Imperative* presents a most compelling case for a new hope of our endangered times in tandem with a new holistic paradigm in understanding the self, the world, and global civic actions based on conscious evolution for life on Earth.

—Dr. Inwon Choue is a political thinker, practitioner in civic agenda, and the Chancellor of Kyung Hee University System, Seoul, South Korea

This book by Ervin Laszlo is fundamental in this moment of environmental crisis which represents a threat to the survival of all of us. His book gifts us in extraordinary ways: it reconnects us with that in-forming field that underlies our existence. Ervin Laszlo is one of the greatest philosophers and writers in the history of science.

—Pier Mario Biava, MD, author of *Information Medicine* and *Cancer and the Search for Meaning*

CONTENTS

OUR COSMIC MISSION

We have reached a critical juncture in our evolution on the planet. Now we face a survival challenge: evolve or perish. If we are to set forth our tenure on Earth, we need to evolve the way we relate to each other and to the planet. This calls for a change in the way we act, which in turn calls for a change in the way we think. This is a crucial, and by no means simple task. How to cope with it is the subject of this book.

We need to wake up to the realization that the problems, the crises and the threats we experience are symptoms of the way we have been, and on the whole still are, thinking and acting. We live in an era of rapid change — an evolution of which the outcome is not yet decided. This is not a biological, but a social and cultural, a human *feeling and perception* evolution.

There is more to evolution than we have been told. The new sciences of life tell us that evolution is not limited to the genetic pool of living species. It is a fundamental process of change and development involving all facets of life on the planet — involving indeed the planet itself. It is not limited to the Earth. It is a universal progression from origins in the chaos of the Big Bang to the order and coherence that now meets our eye — of which conscious human beings are among the most remarkable manifestations.

However, evolution is not a smooth and even process; it unfolds on this planet in a strongly nonlinear fashion. It is continuous, but it is interspersed with radical fluctuations, dramatic fallbacks and positive forward leaps. Its phases of downshift may be followed by a phase of upshift to higher forms and levels of order. We have just lived through a phase of traumatic downshift on the planet. If we are to attain to the phase of a positive upshift, we must survive the impact of the downshift and not fall victim to it.

We are at a tipping-point in our evolution, a watershed that leads either to the extinction of the human species, or to the birth of a planetary civilization where humans live in harmony with each other and with life on Earth.

For a member of a conscious species, purposively guiding its evolution to harmony with life on Earth should not prove to be a utopian venture. It is feasible in principle, and should be feasible in practice. Undertaking it is the human survival imperative. It does not call for manipulating the physical and biological conditions of human life, nor for altering the genetic constitution of the human and other species. It calls for a more evolved and enlightened consciousness, inspired by the evolutionary impetus of living in harmony with life and the universe.

Consciously guiding our evolution to harmony with the symphony of life is the necessary and urgent next step to ensure our tenure on the planet. This is a momentous step, a step of truly cosmic dimensions. Protecting the persistence of a conscious species in the universe is a cosmic mission. When we undertake it, we shall have reached a momentous milestone in our evolution. We can then celebrate the return of harmony and peace on the planet.

PART ONE

PREPARING THE UPSHIFT TO CONSCIOUS EVOLUTION

UPSHIFT! THE WHY, THE WHERE TO, AND THE HOW

CHAPTER 1

THE HISTORIC *OPPORTUNITY*

Shifting up to a better world — or drifting down to crisis and chaos: this, as Hamlet would say, is the question. To pose this question as a real alternative in the world constitutes a nonrecurrent historic opportunity. It is the challenge of the tipping point at which we find ourselves.

The crises we have been experiencing are driving us to change. It is no longer a question of whether to change or not to change, the only question is *how* to change. The wrong way would have catastrophic consequences. We would encounter a series of deepening crises — the virus crisis and the climate crisis would be only forerunners. But the right way could open an era of better life for humanity on the planet. We can still choose the way we go. We can still take our evolution into our own hands.

The Old Testament told us, where there is no vision, the people perish (*Proverbs* 29:18). To live and live well, we need vision. This requirement is sadly lacking in the contemporary world. Helplessness, dejection, and disorientation abound. The vision most people have of the future is of crisis and breakdown. The clouds on the horizon obscure the sun that still shines above in the sky. The sun does shine, but we have to perceive it to be guided by it. It is high time to take a cool look at the world we have created — and take account of what went wrong and consider what we can do to put it right.

Where We Are Today: The Downshift / Upshift Ledger

There are signs that there is a true and spreading awakening in many parts of the globe. Action is generally moving from the local and national to the international and global level. The conditions under which human life can flourish on the planet are becoming known. They are not only better known, but also are increasingly acted upon. The actions contemplated today may or may not be sufficient to shift humankind to a flourishing world — but there is a reasonable expectation that they are constructive, helpful in that regard.

There are persisting problems in our world, as well as positive developments. Let us create a ledger. On the positive side, we can enter that there are major, even global projects to ensure the conditions under which humanity can persist on Earth. The international community is waking up. An unprecedented set of remedial measures is being developed, and major pledges are made to meet the global crisis. Attention is focusing on the United Nation's Sustainable Development Goals, on the climate objectives brought forth by the international climate conferences including COP 26, and on the Resolutions of the G20, the club of industrialized nations. It is becoming clear that reaching these and related objectives is essential for ensuring the persistence of now nearly 8 billion humans on the planet. In less than a century since theologian Hans Küng proclaimed of the founding of the United Nations that there can be "No peace among the nations without peace among the religions," a vibrant global interfaith movement is now in place, convened through innumerable organizations and resulting in influential books by global interfaith leaders including "The Nine Points of

Agreement Among the World's Religions" in *The Common Heart* (2006) and "The Nine Elements of a Universal Spirituality" (2013). A recent international bestseller noting over 100,000 international organizations working for global transformative change is subtitled "How the Largest Movement in the World Came into Being and Why No One Saw it Coming."[1] This is a basically promising development, to be entered on the positive side of our ledger.

On the negative side, devastating conflicts among the world's religious communities continue, as if to belie the seeming progress reported above. Even as we write, humanity is embroiled in over twenty different wars per Wikipedia 's "List of Ongoing World Conflicts."

We must also not fail to note that the financial costs of achieving the goals and objectives proclaimed by well-meaning organizations have not been covered. So far, neither the international community nor the business community have provided or even effectively projected adequate financing. At the same time, the threats keep intensifying, and the costs of dealing with them keep rising.

The fact is that the current level of the pledges is inadequate to cope with the problems. Even if they were adequately financed, the goals to which they are dedicated would not overcome the threats. More is needed to prevent a catastrophic rise of the level of the world's oceans and the aridity of vast tracts of the continents than creating carbon neutral economies by 2050, not to mention only by 2060, and thereby stop global warming at the 1.5 degree Celsius level. Achieving the current goal would not foreclose further negative forms of climate change — it would merely postpone their coming. We need to go beyond the currently targeted solutions and face the facts. We are on the brink of a global survival crisis. This crisis is clearly measurable in regard to the climate. The so-called "climate crisis" is not just a crisis of the climate — of the weather we are having. It is a crisis of our survival on the planet.

According to in-depth climate research by McKay and collaborators, the way our climate is now evolving takes us to the brink of disastrous tipping points. These points have been spelled out by Johan Rockström and his team in reference to the Planetary Boundaries (PB) framework. This framework identifies nine critical processes that regulate the stability and resilience of the Earth System. They identified nine "Planetary Boundaries" within which humanity can continue to live and thrive for generations. A review of these boundaries in 2022 showed that five out of the nine boundaries already have been crossed. This poses an unprecedented threat. The IPCC (Intergovernmental Panel on Climate Change) noted that we are reaching the outermost limits of climate-change adaptation by humanity and many other species and ecosystems.[2]

We are approaching survival-deciding tipping points. We need to shift the trajectory of our evolution from the present trajectory of downshift to a consciously pursued trajectory of upshift.

Where We Are Going

On the positive side of our ledger, we can enter that we now have agreement on a number of crucial goals and objectives, and partial financing to achieve them. But there is also a negative side — while we are moving in the right direction, we are not moving far enough nor fast enough. To meet the challenges of global sustainability, bolder objectives and more adequate financing are needed. Resolutions and projections on national and international levels are no longer sufficient. Action is needed on the global scale, and this presupposes the agreement and active participation of a critical mass of the world's peoples.

The conscious involvement of the people of the world remains a precondition of heading off the advent of unsustainable and ultimately unlivable conditions on the planet. The people factor remains crucial. Notwithstanding the recurrence of dictatorships and the persistently hierarchical way in which power is applied in nationalistic societies, now the overall system of humanity is at least aware of, and appears inherently to prefer, a democratic bottom line. International surveys by PEW, Harris, Yankelovich and *Financial Times* indicate that some 80% of citizens interviewed in the world believe that an ideal society would be democratic. People want a voice in electing their leaders and want to choose the services and products placed on the market by business enterprises. At the same time, the current statistics of Wikipedia's "Democracy Index" show that only about 6% of the world's governments are democracies, and only 30% are moving in a democratic direction. The rest are autocracies or some variety of dictatorships.

The discrepancy between people's aspirations and their actual conditions is a challenge we need urgently to address.[3]

What is actually done to enlist the active engagement of a critical segment of today's people for projects to create sustainable conditions on the planet? For the present, not enough. The engagement of people commands the active attention of concerned scientists and humanists and some social media, but not much more. For lack of a global-level public engagement, the sword of Damocles remains suspended above our heads.

Where we are going from where we are now depends on the recognition by a critical mass of the world's people that we need new thinking — a new way of looking at ourselves and the world. The current levels of local and global unsustainability are the result of a flaw in the current way of thinking. Building an effective political, social, and ecological system to replace the fragmented malfunctioning system now in place calls for a veritable revolution in most people's thinking — and in the actions inspired by that thinking.

Three Assessments

Here are noteworthy assessments of the human condition and its prospects for the future by three awakened and insightful individuals. They merit serious attention. One warns of the dangers that face us, the second calls for an almost messianic revolution, while the third perceives the dangers but places its trust in our power to overcome them.

> "In the face of an absolutely unprecedented emergency, society has no choice but to take dramatic action to avert a collapse of civilization. Either we will change our ways and build an entirely new kind of global society, or they will be changed for us."
> —Gro Harlem Brundtland, former prime minister of Norway, Chair of the World Commission on Environment and Development

> "Ultimately, this Earth can be saved from mankind only if people are prepared to live with nature, rather than upon nature. Recognition of the oneness of life on earth, of its beauty and its sanctity, must be spread by an almost messianic revolution."
> —Sir Mark Oliphant, former governor of South Australia, founding member of the Pugwash Club[4]

> "Here and there in history one notes a sudden concentration of energies, a more favorable constellation of social opportunities, an almost worldwide upsurge of prophetic anticipation, disclosing new possibilities for the race: so it was with the worldwide changes in the sixth century BC symbolized by

> Buddha, Solon, Zoroaster, Confucius, and their immediate successors, changes that gave common values and purposes to people too far separated physically for even Alexander the Great to unite them. Out of still deeper pressures, anxieties, insecurities, a corresponding renewal on an even wider scale now seems open for mankind."
>
> —Lewis Mumford, noted historian, in his classic *The Conduct of Life*

Yes, Madam Brundtland, we are living an unprecedented emergency. Yes, Sir Oliphant, in today's world, a revolution must spread that is almost messianic. And yes, Professor Mumford, we do possess precious, and in the contemporary world still largely ignored, capacities for overcoming the crisis: there is a powerful force in the universe that is *with* us.

Information Note (1): The Crisis Point in the Perspective of the Contemporary Systems Sciences

We have reached a crisis point. If we are to go beyond this point and shift up rather than down, we need know that upshifting is a realistic option. This excursion into contemporary systems theory tells us that it is. We have a real choice *because* we are in crisis. Crisis is not only danger, it is also opportunity — golden opportunity.

Crisis in a system constitutes what in the systems sciences is called a "bifurcation": a forking in the trajectory of the system's evolution. When a complex dynamic system becomes unstable, it is compelled to shift the trajectory of its evolution. The human system is in crisis, and it either bifurcates, or leaves the scene of history.

The opportunity for fundamental change does not appear in a functional system. For fundamental change, a disruption is called for in the system: a critical fluctuation. Fluctuations occur at all times in the system, and when they reach a critical point, the system either shifts its evolutionary trajectory to a more stable branch, or decomposes to its more stable components.

The system in question may be a group of cells in an organism, a species in the biosphere, or a species in the web of life on the planet. The system that concerns us is the latter: the ensemble of the social, economic, and political systems that constitute the system of humanity on the planet. This system is now in the throes of a critical fluctuation — it is critically unstable. Its evolutionary trajectory is on the point of bifurcating. Insightful people have been anticipating that the human system on the planet will sooner or later bifurcate — its trajectory will break down.

Systems scientists have been investigating the dynamics of the process of bifurcation and reached important insights. It turns out that bifurcation is one-way; it cannot be reversed. But it is not predetermined — it allows for choice. Even a small fluctuation within the system can "nucleate" and govern the evolution of the whole system. In today's world there are many fluctuations —tipping points— that decide the choice among various alternatives. Bifurcation in a complex system is governed by "chaotic attractors" — a probabilistic process of change across chaos. This means extreme sensitivity to change, and significant openness in the system to alternative paths of evolution.

Living at the crisis point, we are granted a golden opportunity. Given growing instability in our political, social, and economic systems, even small groups of people can influence the way we go. They can create the small but potent "initial kick" that decides among alternative paths of evolution for our system.

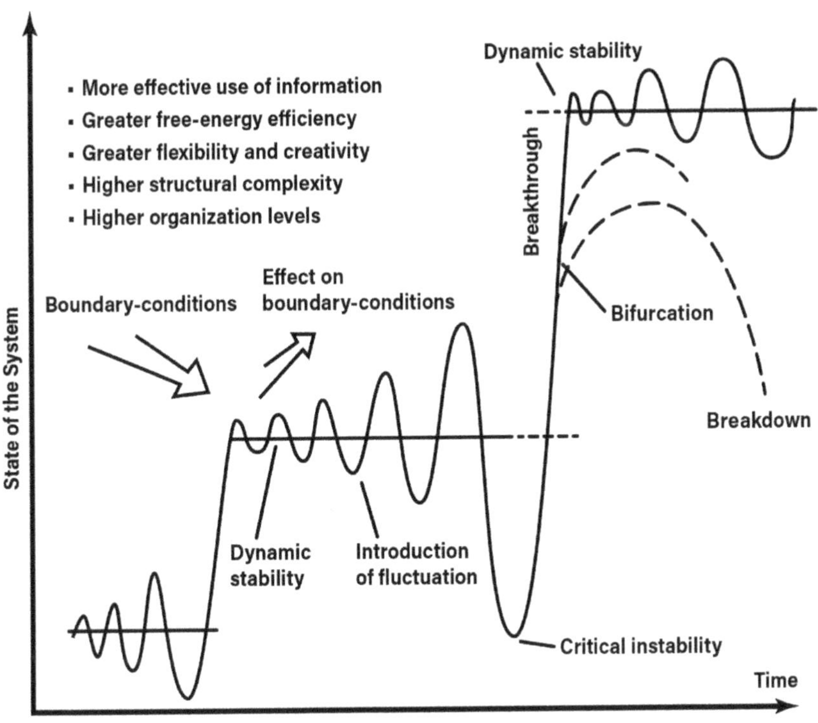

Figure 1

A typical sequence of events in a process of bifurcation. (1) Fluctuations augment in the system. (2) The fluctuations reach a critical threshold where the system no longer returns to its previous state but leaps to a new state of dynamic stability—or breaks down. (3) In interaction with its environment, a series of intensifying fluctuations appear in the system. (4) A fluctuation reaches a further critical threshold—the "tipping point"—and shifts the system to a new state of dynamic stability.

The iteration of the process of bifurcation either leads to the system's demise, or shifts it to higher states and forms of dynamic stability. The resulting system is characterized by a more effective use of information; greater efficiency in the employment of the available resources; greater complexity in structure; and further increase in its levels of organization.

The difference between bifurcation in a system composed of human beings and bifurcation in every other system is the presence of an evolved consciousness. In the human system, the participants can be aware of what is happening and can consciously act to influence it. The decisive actions do not call for the exercise of brute force; they can be created by a shift in the values and beliefs of people. Victor Hugo said that there is nothing as powerful in the world as an idea whose time has come. A shift in the mindset of a critical mass can be powerful enough to decide the way the human system evolves — whether it shifts down to chaos and decay, or up to a more viable condition.

In the absence of the positive "kick," the chances that the human system would evolve toward a more stable condition are slim. A well-placed initial kick in our destabilized system is needed to overcome the remaining, and currently still growing, resistance to change in mainstream society. Because as long as today's society appears salvageable, those who have a significant stake in it are reluctant to abandon it in favor of something new — they fear for their privileges. They would rather try salvaging the system than reaching out to something else. Resistance to change can block the evolution of our system. However, the source of the resistance can be identified, and it can be overcome, or at least mitigated.

Shifting to another branch of our evolution is a disruptive development: it means fundamental change. And fundamental change does not come from the top — it comes from the bottom. The top becomes destabilized and loses its power to govern the system. At first marginal, but then more and more potent changes at the bottom take over the governing of the system.

This is the way evolution works in nature, and it is likely to be the way it unfolds in the system of human communities as well.

CHAPTER 2

WHY WE NEED TO UPSHIFT

We spoke of the necessity of an upshift, but did not name the specific reasons for it. Now we shall do so. What, exactly, are the reasons for launching a movement to upshift the way we live and think on the planet?

Critical Conditions in the Planetary Ecology

In the late twentieth and early twenty-first centuries, conditions of a less and less tractable kind have surfaced in relations between people and nature: between the system of humanity and the planet's ecology. The advent of these conditions has not been accidental; it could have been foreseen. We could have, as we now will, trace the advent of these conditions to the unfolding of two long-term trends:

1. the rapid growth of demand for the planet's physical and biological resources by a growing human population, and

2. the concurrent shrinking and threatening depletion of some of the planet's essential physical and biological resources.

If these trends were to continue to unfold, the curves of their unfolding would cross, and humanity's demand on the resources of the planet would exceed the planet's capacity to meet it. This would create a historically unprecedented condition.

For most of our five-million-year-plus history, humanity's demand in relation to the available resources has not been significant. With primitive technologies and smaller numbers of people, planetary resources seemed limitless. Even when we exhausted a local environment and depleted local resources, there were always other resources and environments to exploit.

But by the middle of the nineteenth century our population reached one billion, and it is over 7.8 billion today. The world population may grow to 10 billion by the middle of this century. Approximately 95 percent of this growth would occur in the presently poor countries and regions, but these regions are not a closed system: their penuries would soon be distributed to all the countries and regions of the globe.

Today's humans constitute only about 0.014 percent of the biomass of life on earth, and 0.44 percent of the biomass of animals. Such a small fragment need not constitute a threat to the entire system, and hence itself. But because of excessive resource use and environmental degradation, we do threaten the global system. Our impact on the earth's resources is entirely out of proportion to our size. We cannot continue to increase our demands without provoking a major dieback of our populations.

One of the most important measures of the human impact on the planet, the "ecological footprint," gives us some estimates. The ecological footprint measures the share of the planet's biological productivity used by an individual, a city, a nation, or all of humanity. It is the area of land required to support a human community. If the footprint of a settlement is larger than the area of that settlement, that settlement is not independently sustainable. A city is intrinsically unsustainable because very few of the natural resources used by its inhabitants come from within its boundaries — most of them (such as food, water, and waste disposal) rely on hinterlands and catchments. But entire regions and countries could well be sustainable: their ecological footprint need not extend beyond their territories. This, however, is not the case. Today, humanity lives beyond its means — it exceeds the capacity of the planet to maintain a supply of breathable air and drinkable water, absorb pollution, and provide room for human habitations and their essential infrastructure.

The situation would be still more dramatic if all countries would adopt socioeconomic development on the Western mold. If the footprint of the more than forty "rich" countries was to be attained by all 193 formally constituted nation-states of the world, the global overshoot would be at least 100 percent. This means that if humanity were to remain in balance with its ecological base, we would have to colonize another planet with endowments similar to Earth.

Our ecological unsustainability is the result of a mode of development as old as human civilization. Prehistoric societies were stable and enduring; they evolved a sustainable relationship with their environment. Only the energy of the sun entered the nature–human system, and only the heat radiated into space left it — everything else was cycled and recycled within it. Food and water came from the local environment and were returned into that environment. Even in death, the human body did not leave the ecology; it entered the soil and contributed to its fertility. Nothing that men and women brought into being accumulated as "nonbiodegradable" toxins; nothing we did caused lasting damage to nature's cycles of generation and regeneration.

The situation changed when groups of early humans learned to manipulate the environment and broke open the loop of regeneration that earlier tribes maintained. With this change, the human impact on the natural environment began its fateful increase.

As better tools were invented, more resources could be accessed, and existing resources could be further exploited. As a result, more people could be supported, and the number of humans on the planet could grow. With the control of fire, perishable foods could be maintained over longer periods, and human settlements spread over the continents.

No longer content to gather and hunt their food, humans learned to plant seeds and use rivers for irrigation and the removal of wastes. They domesticated some species of dogs, horses, and cattle. These practices further increased humanity's impact on nature. Nourishment began to flow from a purposively modified environment, and the growing wastes from larger and technologically more advanced communities continued to disappear conveniently, with smoke vanishing into thin air and solid waste washing downstream in rivers and dispersing in the seas. If a local environment gradually became arid and inhospitable — due to deforestation and overworking the soil — there was always virgin land to conquer and to exploit.

This is no longer the case. Now we are destroying even islands although it is evident that they are finite both in space and in resources.

There is a profound message here. The new science of Island Biogeography shows that continents themselves are actually islands at a large scale. What happens to islands is a harbinger of implications for the continental scale. Easter Island is a case study in point. Its virgin condition appeared protected by thousands of miles of surrounding ocean. It was an ecological paradise with ample natural food for its ancient inhabitants. But just as we have done on the globe's massive continents, its peoples — unknowingly and catastrophically — mismanaged both human population and available resources, starting with deforestation (for fire-building, homes, and the boat building needed for fishing). Innocently, sustainable agriculture and forestry were not employed, and the island and its nearby waters were over-hunted and over-fished. Suddenly, there was a catastrophic crisis of pitting population against resources and a sociological disaster that led even to cannibalism. It is easy to see the parallel with what is happening now across our world's continents. We also understand today that once magnificent, and prolific, city states of ancient times were also "islands" in a larger geography. They, too, when populations surged and resources waned, perished for lack of sustainability and had to be abandoned.

This kind of blind exploitation is happening at alarming rates and with powerful technologies being employed to exploit resources. The island of Nauru is a striking illustration. An island republic of fewer than eleven thousand people, Nauru was a tropical paradise but a few decades ago. Then international mining companies began to extract phosphate, stripping the topsoil. As the price of phosphate rose from ten dollars a ton to over sixty-five dollars, by 1968, the island republic became the second-richest country on earth. But the ecological price has been high: in the span of a few decades, the island became a moonscape of gnarled spiky rock. Its economy has been failing. Its inhabitants turned from eating vegetables and other fresh produce to fatty and salty tinned goods, producing one of the highest levels of obesity, heart disease, and diabetes in the world.

Now the island republic seeks further income from opening up the seabed for exploration — an economically promising scheme as the resources to be won from the sea bottom are becoming more and more valuable, needed for the production of a new generation of batteries and other advanced technologies.

Today, even the deep sea faces the prospect of large-scale human intervention. The results, experts admit, are hardly foreseeable.

Due to "in-sane" and irresponsible interventions in the delicately balanced ecology of the planet, we are now approaching the outer limits of the earth's capacity to sustain human life. This capacity is becoming more and more reduced due to irresponsible interventions. This fact is obscured — and purposively disregarded — by the short-term economic gains offered by the interventions. The price is clearly evident in the field of agriculture. Chemically bolstered mechanized agriculture is a lucrative enterprise, it increases yields per acre and makes more acres available for cultivation, but it also increases the growth of algae that chokes lakes and waterways. Chemicals such as DDT are effective insecticides, but they poison entire animal, bird, and insect populations.

Waste disposal contributes to the reduction of the planet's human carrying capacity. We discard not only our biological wastes into the environment. We inject over one hundred thousand chemical compounds into the land, rivers, and seas; dump millions of tons of sludge and solid waste into the oceans; release billions of tons of CO_2 into the air; and increase the level of radioactivity in water, land, and air.

The wastes we discard into the environment do not vanish; they plague people near and far, including those who produce them. Refuse dumped into the sea returns to poison marine life and infest entire coastal regions. In the industrialized countries, over a million chemicals are bubbling through the groundwater systems, and in many countries, even in the least developed ones, rivers and lakes have up to a hundred times the acceptable level of pollutants. The smoke rising from homesteads and factories does not dissolve and disappear — the released CO_2 remains in the atmosphere and affects weather the world over. Not surprisingly, there has been a massive increase in allergies in both urban and rural populations. The appellations of toxic environmental effects constitute a whole new vocabulary: there is MCS (multiple chemical sensitivity), wood preservative syndrome, solvent intolerance, chemically associated immune dysfunction, clinical ecology syndrome, chronic fatigue syndrome, fibromyalgia, sick-building syndrome, and many more.

Unsustainable Conditions in Our Social and Economic Systems

The advent of unsustainable relations between the system of humanity and the planetary ecology has been accompanied by the advent of critical conditions in humanity's social and economic systems. The population of the planet is exposed to growing strain and stress. While economic, ecologic, and technological globalization proceeds at a breakneck pace, a third of the economies of the world are left out of it. The worldwide system of states has been growing together in some respects — first and foremost in trade and communication — but it has been coming apart in the social and economic field.

As already noted, pursuing economic growth without checks and balances is a dangerous option. Economic growth has been made possible by the spread of information and communication technologies, and the dynamism of the private sector. But this high-impact process did not produce well distributed benefits. Many states and economies have been left out of it, and their populations have been resentful, often turning violent.

The underprivileged segments of the population have been facing less and less tenable conditions. The nodes of poverty have been expanding, increasing the gap between rich and poor. The so-called Gini coefficient, a measure of the rich–poor gap, has been growing. The poor countries and poor populations have been hit hardest by the crisis and the recession it created. Vast populations have been pushed to the very limits of physical subsistence.

The gap between rich and poor also has been growing *within* given states and regions. The poor segments of most countries have been growing, and their poverty has increased. This is a major injustice, and the poor countries and populations are deeply resenting it, sparking an ever more violent protest movement.

There is good reason to protest. If access to the planet's physical and biological resources were evenly distributed, all people and populations could be supported. If food supplies, for example, were equally accessible, every person would receive about a hundred calories more than what is required to replace the 1,800 to 3,000 calories each normal person expends every day (the average healthy diet is about 2,600 calories). But people in the rich countries of North America, Western Europe, and Japan obtain 140 percent of the caloric requirements of a normal healthy life, whereas people in the poorest countries, such as Madagascar, Guyana, and Laos, are limited to only 70 percent.

The world's pattern of energy consumption is just as disparate. The averages tell the story. The average energy consumption in Africa has been half a kilowatt hour of commercial electrical energy, while the corresponding average in Asia and Latin America has been 2–3 kWh. The average in North America, Europe and Australia rose to 8 kWh. With 4.1 percent of the world population, the United States alone has been consuming 25 percent of the world's commercial energy.

Affluent and wasteful consumption in the rich parts of the world is not the only cause of the crisis of the international system; the way poor people often obtain the resources required for their survival is unsustainable in itself. The more than a billion and a half people who, according to World Bank estimates, live at or below the absolute poverty line (defined as the equivalent of one dollar a day) destroy the environment on which they vitally depend. This creates a major demographic unbalance. With rural environments degrading, people abandon their native towns and villages and flee to the cities.

Urban complexes have experienced explosive growth — one out of fewer than three people now lives in a city, and by the middle of the century, two out of every three people will do so. By then, there would be more than five hundred cities with populations of over one million, and thirty megacities exceeding eight million. Such cities cannot be self-sustaining; their ecological footprint vastly exceeds their territory. The bigger they are, the greater their dependence on their hinterlands.

Social and cultural disparities and conflicts have been stressing life in most societies. Traditional social structures have been breaking down; the family, as sociologists say, has become "defunctionalized." The traditional functions of family life have been taken over by institutions dominated by outside interests. Child-rearing has been increasingly entrusted to kindergartens and company or community daycare centers. Leisure-time activities have been dominated by the marketing and PR campaigns of commercial enterprises, and the provision of daily nourishment has shifted from the family kitchen to supermarkets, prepared food industries, and fast-food chains.

In cities, the exigencies of economic survival and the striving for a higher standard of living have broken apart the traditional extended family, and in regions of extreme poverty, even the nuclear family has proven difficult to keep together. To make ends meet, women and children have had to leave the homestead and search for ways to generate money. Women have been extensively exploited, given menial jobs for low pay, and young people have fared even worse. More than fifty million children have been forced into manual labor, often for a pittance, working in factories, mines, and on the land. Many are forced to live on the streets as "self-employed vendors," a euphemism for beggars.

An even more deplorable consequence of family poverty has been the letting go, and sometimes the outright selling, of children into prostitution. UNICEF called this "one of the most abusive, exploitative, and hazardous forms of child labor." In Asia alone, one million children are believed to work as juvenile prostitutes, exploited by the highly profitable and growing industries of international pedophilia, fueled by widespread sex tourism.

Whether in the cities or in the countryside, poverty has been characterized by malnutrition, joblessness, and unjust and degrading conditions of life. At the same time, it has made for the overworking of productive lands, the contamination of rivers and lakes, and the lowering of water tables. This has created a vicious cycle. Poverty prompted poor families to have many children because children can help families at the level of subsistence to garner the resources needed for their survival. The resulting growth of poor populations has both inflicted further damage on the environment, and destroyed the kinship structures that provide the stability of traditional societies.

The Bottom Line

Conducting our business on the planet as "business-as-usual" created a world that is ecologically unsustainable and socially and economically crisis prone. The poor populations are locked into a vicious cycle of poverty creating depressed conditions, and depressed conditions expanding the nodes of poverty. In turn, the more affluent segments find themselves living and working under conditions of no-holds-barred competition and job uncertainty, producing more and more anxiety and stress. The specter of deepening crises appears ever more insistently on the horizon.

The business of business-as-usual proved to be a fatal business; it created an unsustainable, unjust, and crisis-prone world. Now, when the global crisis grants us the opportunity to build a different world, it's time to ask ourselves: Is the world of business-as-usual the world we want to keep? Is it the world we want to hand down to our children?

In the end, this may be a moot question. We are living in the midst of the sixth mass extinction, known as the Anthropocene extinction, as it is triggered by humans. Since the middle of the twentieth century, more than 60 percent of the animal species on the planet have disappeared, and according to some ecologists, the remaining 40 percent may follow in not much more than twenty years. That could lead to the destabilization and eventual collapse of the global ecosystem. The dinosaurs disappeared after millions of years of reign following the collapse of the global ecosystem (probably due to the impact of a giant meteorite), and our arbitrary interventions in the planet's ecology could have similar consequences for *Homo sapiens* — who would then prove to be not sapient at all.

But we are not extinct yet, and we could change direction. There is no way back, and there is no future in continuing on the way we have been going. But there is a way forward, and we could enter on it.

We shall depict the principal features of a sustainable and peaceful world in the chapters that follow, and we can already note its key features. Unlike the world we have created, a sustainable and peaceful world exists in harmony with the web of life on the planet. If we are to reach such a world, we need to take in hand our own evolution. We can no longer trust in the serendipity of random interactions creating positive changes, nor in the good intentions of some concerned individuals. We need to make our evolution on Earth a conscious, purposively envisaged and implemented enterprise.

CHAPTER 3

TO *WHERE* ARE WE TO UPSHIFT

We urgently need a global upshift because we have created unsustainable conditions on the planet. We have lived irresponsibly, and in some cases literally "in-sanely," damaging the integrity of nature and of our communities. The time has come to adopt a wiser, saner way of living. This calls for a change in the way we think, inspiring the needed changes in the way we act and live.

In the past, new ways of thinking and living evolved over many generations. The rhythm of change was relatively slow and allowed people to adapt their relations to each other and their attitudes toward their environment. These times have passed. The crucial period for finding our way to better thinking and living is now compressed not just into the lifetime of the living generations, but into the span of a few years. We could afford the luxury of moving forward through trial and error in the past, but we cannot afford to do so today. We need to know where we want to go, and how we can go.

Climate change and the virus pandemic came on top of a number of critical conditions in the social, economic, and ecological domain. If not checked, these conditions would give rise to still more serious conditions: to deepening local and global crises.

The overexploitation of resources and the impairment of nature, coupled with the unequal distribution of wealth and power, call for fundamental change. The way forward is not a return to the way already traveled, to the world of business-as-usual. It is a different way.

A better way is very different from the way we have travelled. Lao Tzu warned, "*If you do not change direction, you may end up where you're heading." Today, this* would be disastrous. The business of business-as-usual has been heading us toward socially, economically, and ecologically untenable conditions. Without a change in direction, we would be on the way to a world of increasing population pressure and spreading poverty; to growing social and political confrontation; to industry- and lifestyle-created climate change; to food and energy shortages; and to a worsening industrial, urban, and agricultural pollution of air, water, and soil. We would encounter more frequent and ever more devastating floods and tornadoes triggered by an unbalanced climate, and higher rates of mortality due to exposure to accumulated quantities of toxins in soil, air, and water.

We cannot afford to be further exposed to such conditions. We need fundamental change in the way we act, and that means a fundamental change in the way we think. And that means fundamental change in the way we grow and evolve.

The Nature of the Consciousness to Which We Are to Upshift

The Germans have an expression that is widely used, even in other languages. It is *Weltanschauung*. This is more than the view of the world based on science, or on any other doctrine or source. It is the ensemble of one's views of who he is, and what his world is, encompassing all of one's values and beliefs. It is what today we refer to as "our consciousness."

Until recently, people in societies rich and poor, Western and Eastern, lived and acted with an outdated consciousness. Most people were, and largely still are, mesmerized by the prospect of hoarding and accumulating material goods, personal wealth, and leading an ostentatious and wasteful "modern" way of living. People thought, and still think, that the way they think and act is scientifically grounded. Individuals, they believe, have little or no influence on the way the world is going; consequently, there is no need for individuals to feel responsible for the shape of the world. They hold on to the notion that life is a struggle for survival and that claiming otherwise is to indulge in wishful thinking. They see "survival of the fittest" as a law that holds sway in nature and that there is no sense in contesting it. Further, in any event, they believe that an "invisible hand" (the hand of the free market) will sooner or later distribute the benefits.

The spread of this obsolete way of thinking and living has led to the critical conditions we have discussed in the ecological, social, and economic systems. It is high time to realize that this consciousness is flawed: the world is not a giant mechanism operating according to rigid laws. In the real world, the future is determined by how we perceive the world, and how we act in it. Today, the future hinges on the way we act in our unstable and unsustainable social, economic, and ecological systems. How the world evolves is not decided by laws but by our values and behaviors. We know that the future will not be the same as the past, and not even as the present. It will be a different world that could be better or worse than the world today.

Fortunately, we can still evolve the way we think. We can learn to act on the requirement for an adapted consciousness, and use our adapted consciousness to guide the way we evolve.

The Clarion Calls[5]

1. *The Call for Creativity and Diversity*

A new way of thinking has become the necessary condition for responsible living and acting. Evolving it means fostering creativity in all people, in all parts of the world. Creativity is not a genetic but a cultural endowment of human beings. Culture and society change fast, while genes change slowly: no more than one half of one percent of the human genetic endowment is likely to alter in an entire century. Hence, most of our genes date from the Stone Age or before; they could help us to live in the jungles of nature but not in the jungles of civilization. Today's economic, social, and technological environment is our own creation, and only the creativity of our mind — our culture, spirit, and consciousness — could enable us to cope with it. Genuine creativity does not remain paralyzed when faced with unusual and unexpected problems but confronts them openly, without prejudice. Cultivating it is a precondition of finding our way toward a globally interconnected society in which individuals, enterprises, states, and the whole family of peoples and nations could live together peacefully, cooperatively, and with mutual benefit.

Sustained diversity is another requirement of our age. Diversity is basic to all things in nature and in art: a symphony cannot be made of one tone or even played by one instrument; a painting must have many shapes and perhaps many colors; and a garden is more beautiful if it contains flowers and plants of many different kinds. A multicellular organism cannot survive if it is reduced to one kind of cell — even sponges evolve cells with specialized functions. And more complex organisms have cells and organs of a great variety, with a great variety of mutually complementary and exquisitely coordinated functions. Cultural and spiritual diversity in the human world is just as essential as diversity in nature and in art. A human community must have members that are different from one another not only in age and sex; but also in personality, color, and creed. Only then could its members perform the tasks that each does best, and complement each other so that the whole formed by them could grow and evolve. The evolving global society would have great diversity, were it not for the unwanted and undesirable uniformity introduced through the domination of a handful of cultures and societies. Just as the diversity of nature is threatened by cultivating only one or a few varieties of crops and husbanding only a handful of species of animals, so the diversity of today's world is endangered by the domination of one, or at the most a few, varieties of cultures and civilizations.

The world of the twenty-first century will be viable only if it maintains essential elements of the diversity that has always hallmarked cultures, creeds, economic, social, and political orders, as well as ways of life. Sustaining diversity does not mean isolating peoples and cultures from one another: it calls for international and intercultural contact and communication with due respect for each other's differences, beliefs, lifestyles, and ambitions. Sustaining diversity also does not mean preserving inequality, for equality does not reside in uniformity, but in the recognition of the equal value and dignity of all peoples and cultures. Creating a diverse yet equitable and intercommunicating world calls for more than just paying lip-service to equality and just tolerating each other's differences. Letting others be what they want "as long as they stay in their corner of the world" and letting them do what they want "as long as they don't do it in my backyard" are well-meaning but inadequate attitudes. As the diverse organs in a body, diverse peoples and cultures need to work together to maintain the whole system in which they are a part, a system that is the human community in its planetary abode. In the last decade of the twentieth century, different nations and cultures must develop the compassion and the solidarity that could enable all of us to go beyond the stance of passive tolerance, to actively work with and complement each other.

2. *The Call for Responsibility*

In the course of the twentieth century, people in many parts of the world have become conscious of their rights as well as of many persistent violations of them. This development is important, but in itself it is not enough. In the remaining years of this century, we must also become conscious of the factor without which neither rights nor other values can be effectively safeguarded: our individual and collective responsibilities. We are not likely to grow into a peaceful and cooperative human family unless we become responsible social, economic, political, and cultural actors.

We human beings need more than food, water, and shelter; more even than remunerated work, self-esteem, social acceptance. We also need something to live for: an ideal to achieve, a responsibility to accept. Since we are aware of the consequences of our actions, we can and must accept responsibility for them. Such responsibility goes deeper than many of us may think. In today's world, all people, no matter where they live and what they do, have become responsible for their actions: as private individuals; citizens of a country; collaborators in business and the economy; members of the human community; and persons endowed with mind and consciousness. As individuals, we are responsible for seeking our interests in harmony with, and not at the expense of, the interests and wellbeing of others; for condemning and averting any form of killing and brutality; for not bringing more children into the world than we truly need and can support; and for respecting the right to life, development, and equal status and dignity of all the children, women, and men who inhabit the earth. As citizens of our country, we are responsible for demanding that our leaders beat swords into ploughshares and relate to other nations peacefully and in a spirit of cooperation; that they recognize the legitimate aspirations of all communities in the human family; and that they do not abuse sovereign powers to manipulate people and the environment for shortsighted and selfish ends. As collaborators in business and actors in the economy, we are responsible for ensuring that corporate objectives do not center uniquely on profit and growth, but include a concern that products and services respond to human needs and demands without harming people and impairing nature; that they do not serve destructive ends and unscrupulous designs; and that they respect the rights of all entrepreneurs and enterprises who compete fairly in the global marketplace.

As members of the human community, it is our responsibility to adopt a culture of nonviolence, solidarity, and economic, political, and social equality, promoting mutual understanding and respect among people and nations whether they are like us or different, demanding that all people everywhere should be empowered to respond to the challenges that face them with the material as well as the spiritual resources that are required for this unprecedented task. And as persons endowed with mind and consciousness, our responsibility is to encourage comprehension and appreciation for the excellence of the human spirit in all its manifestations, and for inspiring awe and wonder for a cosmos that brought forth life and consciousness and holds out the possibility of its continued evolution toward ever-higher levels of insight, understanding, love, and compassion.

3. *The Call for Planetary Consciousness*

In most parts of the world, the real potential of human beings is sadly underdeveloped. The way children are raised depresses their faculties for learning and creativity, and the way young people experience the struggle for material survival results in frustration and resentment. In adults, this leads to a variety of compensatory, addictive, and compulsive behaviors. The result is the persistence of social and political oppression, economic warfare, cultural intolerance, crime, and disregard for the environment. Eliminating social and economic ills and frustrations calls for considerable socioeconomic development, and that is not possible without better education, information, and communication. These, however, are blocked by the absence of socioeconomic development so that a vicious cycle is produced: underdevelopment creates frustration, and frustration, giving rise to defective behaviors, blocks development.

This cycle must be broken at its point of greatest flexibility, and that is the development of the spirit and consciousness of human beings. Achieving this objective does not preempt the need for socioeconomic development with all its financial and technical resources, but calls for a parallel mission in the spiritual field. Unless people's spirit and consciousness evolve to the planetary dimension, the processes that stress the globalized society–nature system will intensify and create a shock wave that could jeopardize the entire transition toward a peaceful and cooperative global society. This would be a setback for humanity and a danger for everyone. Evolving human spirit and consciousness is the first vital cause shared by the whole of the human family.

In our world, static stability is an illusion; the only permanence is in sustainable change and transformation. There is a constant need to guide the evolution of our societies so as to avoid breakdowns and progress toward a world where all people can live in peace, freedom, and dignity. Such guidance does not come from teachers and schools, not even from political and business leaders, though their commitment and roles are important. Essentially and crucially, it comes from each person himself and herself. An individual endowed with planetary consciousness recognizes his or her role in the evolutionary process and acts responsibly in light of this perception. Each of us must start with himself or herself to evolve his or her consciousness to this planetary dimension; only then can we become responsible and effective agents of our society's change and transformation.

Planetary consciousness is the knowing as well as the feeling of the vital interdependence and essential oneness of humankind, and the conscious adoption of the ethics and the ethos that this entails. Its evolution is the new imperative of human survival on this planet.

CHAPTER 4

"May the force be with you!"
—*Star Wars* greeting

HOW WE CAN UPSHIFT TO CONSCIOUS EVOLUTION

Go with the Force!

To shed light on the forces that decide our future, we need to go beyond the bounds of mainstream science and consider the existence of a force that is real, yet not recognized in science — at least, until recently. This is the force of evolution. Young people speak of this force, and greet each other with the advice to go with it.

The force that empowers evolution is not science fiction; rather, it is avant-garde science. It is a subtle force, an inclination, an almost spiritual leaning. In the language of the life sciences, it is "a tropism," an attraction toward particular resources or conditions. In the context we adopt here, which is that of the systems sciences, we identify it as a "tropism-generating attractor." Attractors are conceptual tools for measuring the state of a complex system, assessing the configuration of the forces that maintain it and evolve it.

The attractor active in the universe is a subtle bias for particular outcomes among otherwise nondirectional or possibly random interactions. This bias is toward the formation of integral ensembles of diverse elements — complex and coherent entities. They possess a degree and form of integration that amounts to "wholeness." The attractor that biases interactions in the universe is wholeness-oriented: it is a "holotropic attractor." It is not necessarily a separate, additional law of nature: it could be, and most plausibly is, the combined effect of the laws science already has recognized.

The holotropic attractor appears as a tropism toward coherence and oneness throughout nature. In the human realm, it is present on the level of instinct and intuition, or subtle spiritual insight. It connects the individual with nature and the universe. It is effective whether we are aware of it or not. But it is more effective when we are aware of it because then we can consciously align with it.

The existence of an evolutionary bias or tropism in nature is an ancient insight; it is not discovered, but *rediscovered* today. The implications of this rediscovery are profound. They suggest that the evolution of life is not a response to external conditions, but the unfolding of an attraction intrinsic to the universe. There is evidence to support this rediscovery.

Now we know that for nearly two hundred thousand years, the human genome has been essentially the same as it is today. The genes responsible for the functioning of our organism, coding such advanced faculties as articulated speech and a self-reflective mind, are being identified. These genes have been part of our genetic makeup for two hundred thousand years or more. They were present in our genome *before* the faculties they code would have been expressed in our phenome (our biological organism). How come they were part of our genome? Their presence could not have been due to the interaction of many generations with the world around them: they *predate* such interactions. Their presence is also unlikely to be due to a serendipitous series of chance interactions, as the probability of their being constituted by random interactions is astronomically negative. Not just two hundred thousand years, but the 3.5 to 4 billion years that elapsed since the beginning of life on the planet would not be sufficient to provide a reasonable probability that our genes would have been created by a random rearrangement of their cells and molecules.

The conclusion is clear. There is a force in the universe — a tropism or attractor — that biases nonrandom interactions toward forming complex entities, entities that are coherent and can maintain themselves and evolve toward higher levels of coherence and complexity. This force must have been present in the universe at the time the first ensembles of quanta formed in the primeval "soup" of the early universe. Quantum physics discloses that neutral atoms, the structural basis for molecular and macromolecular ensembles, did not arise from random processes: the universe has been "programmed" from its very beginnings to produce complex and coherent entities. These entities emerge whenever and wherever conditions are suitable to form the complex chains of carbon on which life is based. As the surprisingly widespread presence of the "extremophiles" testifies, life emerges even in such unlikely places as the bottom of the sea, near active volcanoes, and in the vicinity of active stars. It emerges under conditions of high salinity, extreme aridity, and nearly lethal levels of radiation.

The insight we now come to is that evolution in the universe is neither random, nor externally generated. It is catalyzed by a cosmic evolutionary force: a tropism or attractor present in space and time, and hence present in every living being. This is "The Force" young people wish to be with them. The cosmic attractor is that force, and it is "with" them, the same as it is "with" all forms of life in the universe.

Science fiction, as well as ancient wisdom, are often the precursors of legitimate science, and legitimate science often rediscovers creative fiction and ancient wisdom. This is the case in regard to the tropism inherent in the universe. The existence of this force is re-stated today in imaginative fiction, and it was recognized in the spiritual traditions for thousands of years. It was articulated by Lao Tzu in the first century AD. The twenty-first verse of the *Tao Te Ching* tells us that:

The Great Virtue is to follow the Tao and only the Tao.
The Tao is shadowy and intangible.
Intangible and evasive, and yet within it is a form.
Evasive and intangible, and yet within it is a substance.
Shadowy and dark, and yet within it is a vital force.
This vital force is real and can be relied upon.

In the thirteenth century, the Japanese Buddha Nichiren Daishonin called the vital force inherent in things "the mystic truth." In his *On Attaining Buddhahood in This Lifetime*, he wrote:

If you wish to free yourself from the sufferings of birth and death you have endured since time without beginning and to attain without fail unsurpassed enlightenment in this lifetime, you must perceive the mystic truth that is originally inherent in all living beings.

The rediscovery of the evolutionary force in the universe brings us essential wisdom at today's crisis point. It tells us that there is a force for coherence and wholeness in nature that we can go with. It is beyond question that going with this force is in our best and most urgent interest.

The Conscious Evolution Scenario

The unfolding of a positive, sustainable and life-promoting development — the scenario of a potent movement for conscious evolution — depends on the emergence of a critical mass of awakened and responsible individuals. Let us assume that this critical mass emerges in time. What kind of development could we expect to experience then?

The first step in this development is likely to be a fresh effort on the part of a growing groups of insightful political and business leaders to safeguard the vital balances of the biosphere. They impose more effective regulations to halt the dumping of CO_2 and other noxious waste products into the environment. As the measures bring fruit, the regulations find more and more support. Public bodies and private enterprises comply with the new regulations not only because noncompliance entails heavy penalties, but also because there is a growing realization that they are necessary.

Together with the regulations required to moderate the threatening aspects of climate change, governments redouble efforts to control the spread of infectious diseases. Coordinated measures are put into practice to liberate the population from the threat of further pandemics.

As the worldwide coordinated measures begin to produce results, people begin to think differently. A sense of urgency to live and act responsibly is joined with a renewed commitment to build a more crisis-resistant world. With the new mindset, people come to see the planet as a living organism of which they are an integral part. This organism, they see, is under mounting stress, and in the absence of adequate measures, humans are becoming an endangered species.

Young people, and sensitive and concerned individuals of all ages, realize that we are a vital element in a system of great complexity and high but increasingly unstable coherence. They realize that this system has been subverted, its evolution derailed. But they also realize that effective constraints are required to avert a downshift into critical and ultimately irreversible conditions that make society prone to a series of catastrophic breakdowns.

Before long, action prompted by fear of the consequences of inaction is replaced by action inspired by the perception of the positive possibilities. The stages of the evolutionary upshift are marked by a sequence of progressive developments:

- Seizing the opportunity to change and to transform, people pull together. There is growing support for public policies that exhibit a higher level of social and ecological responsibility. Funds and capital are beginning to be channeled from "defense" and "security" objectives and serving the affluent minority, to the basic needs of the great majority.

- Measures are progressively implemented to safeguard the environment, create an effective system of food and resource distribution, and develop and put to work sustainable energy, transport, and agricultural technologies.

- More and more people gain access to food, jobs, and education. More and more enter interactive platforms on the internet and become active in spreading a dialogue that shapes people's thinking and affects their behavior. Their dialogue prompts them to join together, and together they discover more and more areas of common interest.

- Business leaders begin to change their operating modalities. They work toward creating a circular economy, responsible living on natural income rather than on spending its natural capital. Natural capital, they realize, consists of the riches we borrow from the earth, and these need to be repaid and not just used and discarded. When natural capital is depleted, the community or enterprise based on it goes bankrupt — incapable of maintaining its essential resource base. Drawing on natural income, on the other hand, means using renewable and recyclable energies and substances, and infinite or nearly infinite flow-energies such as wind, tide, and solar energy inflow. These resources have no expiration date, and the enterprises and communities based on them are indefinitely sustainable.

- A corresponding change takes place regarding the way other natural resources are used. The objective is no longer to optimize labor productivity (previously the principal goal of business companies), but to optimize resource productivity. Instead of squeezing the maximum out of every kilogram of matter and kilowatt of energy, the aspiration becomes to design resource-processing systems that require a minimum of nonrenewable materials and a maximum of quasi-infinitely available flow-energies.

- In time, the human community of the planet rises to the challenge of eliminating the specter of deepening crises. Technologically advanced economies pioneer sustainable resource processing systems to operate in the framework of sweeping social and political reforms.

People begin to live more responsibly. A higher level of cooperation among communities, governments, and business companies ensures a more rational consumption of resources and a more efficient discarding of the wastes, thus reducing the human impact on the global ecosystem.

There is less stress within the social and political community itself. National, international, and intercultural animosity, ethnic conflict, racial oppression, economic inequity, and gender inequality diminish. A unilateral focus on satisfying national, corporate, and in-group interests is replaced by wider and less partisan politics: a politics dedicated to meeting the legitimate ends of two of the three Ps: People and Planet. The third P, Profit, is no longer an end in itself — it is a means to an end. The end is the creation of a thriving world on the Planet for the third and most crucial of the three Ps: People.

Information Note (2): The Origins and Unfolding of Evolution in the Universe and on Earth

The holotropic attractor that manifests in our experience, we have said, is the effect of a wholeness-oriented force or impetus on our world. Now we add that this concept is firmly rooted in contemporary cosmology. In the quantum physics cosmology developed by David Bohm, it is viewed as the imprint of the underlying "implicate order" on the manifest "explicate order." This imprint is subtle but effective. It is the attraction to, or tendency for, wholeness and coherence that biases otherwise random interactions in the universe. Interactions in the explicate order are nonrandom; they are oriented to produce complex and coherent systems. It is the bias that makes for a universe of whole-systems evolving on multiple levels of structure and organization.

The transfer of the wholeness and coherence-orienting impetus from the implicate to the explicate order is the meaning of the term "holomovement." In the absence of the holomovement, the universe would be a random swirl of inert plasma without structure and order. The fact that there are coherent systems in the universe is due to the effect of the implicate order on the explicate order.

The effect conveyed by the holomovement is best characterized as an "attractor." Attractors are dynamic factors that account for coherence in complex systems. They may be stationary or steady-state, or dynamic, exhibiting periodicity, or even "strange" or "chaotic" — but not without intrinsic coherence (in this instance, chaos does not mean lack of order, only a complex and intractable variety of order).

There is compelling evidence for the presence of an attractor in the universe, as we shall explain below. The key fact is that not enough time has elapsed since the Big Bang for random interactions to have created the complex and coherent systems we observe. The 13.8-billion-year dimension of that interval does not offer a reasonable probability that random processes would have created the DNA of a fruit fly, much less the complex architectures of living organisms. The conclusion is inescapable: there was, and is, something other than mere chance underlying interactions in the universe.

The story of the universe is not the story recounted by classical physics — it is not based on random interactions producing the phenomena we observe. There is guidance in the way the universe evolves, even if it is intrinsic and not extrinsic to the universe. It took 13.8 billion years for the systems that emerged in space and time to achieve the complexity and coherence that now meets our eye, and this evolution was far more rapid than the evolution that random interactions could have produced. It began following the release of the energies by the singularity known as the Big Bang (we should note that according to "pulsating universe" theories, the Big Bang was not a singularity, but a phase in the pulsation of the underlying cosmic field). These energies produced increasingly ordered and stable systems — units of in-phase vibration that could maintain themselves in the chaos of the early universe. They were *leptons* (electrons, muons, tau particles and neutrinos), *mesons* (pions) and *hadrons* (baryons including protons and neutrons). In the course of time, they clustered into atoms, and the atoms clustered into molecules and molecular assemblies. On the astronomical level, stars and stellar systems and entire galaxies came about.

That evolution would be a universal process is now recognized, but it is not clear what is responsible for it. French philosopher Henri Bergson speculated that it is an *elan vital* that counters the trend toward energy-degradation in natural systems, and biologist Hans Driesch suggested that it is a counter-entropic drive he termed *entelechy*. Philosophers Teilhard de Chardin and Erich Jantsch postulated a dynamic tendency called *syntony*, and others spoke of the structuring factor as *syntropy*. Eastern thinkers call the energy that drives the evolutionary process *prana*, a Sanskrit term, and in the West, psychoanalyst Carl Reich suggested the term *orgone*. Rudolf Steiner called it *etheric force*.

Newton himself recognized the presence of a dynamic, creative factor in the universe and sought to accommodate it in his theory. Mechanistic laws, he admitted, are not full descriptions of reality; they need to be completed with the recognition of what he called an "enlivening and ensouling spirit in all things"— an "animating" or "enlivening" spirit of "vegetation." We now know that this force or factor is a universal attractor shaping the processes unfolding in space and time.

In her book, *The Story of Gaia*, cosmologist Jude Currivan affirms that the universe is a nonlocally unified entity embodying the universal impulse to evolve. This impulse, she claims, arises from a coherence-producing attraction for wholeness and coherence. Evolution is not driven by random mutations, but by all-pervasive coherence-oriented relationships, processes and flows of information.

Currivan reports with regard to the "right first time" structure of the DNA (which has been the genetic template for biological organisms since their first appearance some 4 billion years ago) that the analysis of a million randomized codes has shown that DNA is singularly the best structure in attaining enormous accuracy and maximizing its own ability to build and repair the organism's viability. The assumption that random mutations are the primary driver of evolution is fundamentally flawed.

Building from the emergence of prebiotic and organic life-forms, substantial contingencies, redundancies, checks, balances, and corrections in the genetic replication processes to synthesize cellular structures, go to extraordinary lengths to reduce coding errors and so minimize the possibilities of random mutations. From an estimated error rate in human protein synthesis of one in ten thousand copies in transcribing the initial DNA instructions, further controls such as the coding of the transferred messages, reduces the error rate to a miniscule one in more than a billion copies.

It appears that the highest priority of the organism is to sustain its coherence and integrity, while remaining open and capable of proactively adapting to changing conditions. The effort to retain integrity increases with the complexity of the organism. Thus, while single-celled organisms have "fluid" genomes, being promiscuous in sharing their DNA to access a variety of environmental niches, multicelled species progressively trade off and balance their bodily flexibility with overall structural viability.[6]

The key insight is confirmed with every new discovery in the sciences of life. We and other living beings are not, and cannot be, the product of random processes. An evolution-directed universe brought us forth, and continually guides us to evolve toward wholeness, coherence and complexity.

PART TWO

THE SHIFT TO CONSCIOUS EVOLUTION

A PERSONAL GUIDE TO INFORMED ACTION

CHAPTER 5

"Even the longest journey begins with the first step."
—Chinese folk saying

TAKE THE FIRST STEP

In the perspective of everyday common sense, the first step toward creating an upshift to conscious evolution is to identify and deal with the concrete global and local problems that have come our way. For example, to reduce our consumption of nonrenewable resources, recycle our renewable resources, clean up our seas and waterways, deal with war, violence and criminality, and undertake the most pressing of the myriad problems on the economic, social and political horizon. Yet, by calling for an upshift to conscious evolution, we seem to treat the concrete problems we face as secondary issues — problems of thinking rather than of being and wellbeing.

There is, however, good reason for identifying a new way of thinking as the necessary means for upshifting to a more conscious way of evolving on the planet. The truth is that common sense's concrete problems have deeper causes, and to treat the concrete problems alone is not enough — that is to treat the symptoms alone. This guide to informed action tells you that as a conscious and responsible member of the human community, you must address the causes. The causes lie in your way of acting, which in turn is inspired and influenced by your way of thinking. If you are to overcome the problems we face in common, you must address your way of thinking.

The first step is for you to realize that the thinking that has led you and the bulk of contemporary society to the problems we face needs to be changed. As it is, it leads you and the human family to a dead end. You need to change direction and help others to do so. This calls for being clear about the goals you set for yourself to achieve — about where and how you want to go.

1. Be Clear About the Way to Go

If you are to change to a better way to go, you must have a good working understanding of the world in which you are going. We have said, and we need to repeat: today's world is fundamentally, and in some respects even intrinsically, unsustainable. This means that attempts to sustain it in the way it is are condemned to fail, even if they are technically and politically "realistic." They may be realistic in the short term, but their realism evaporates when we look but a few years ahead.

Patching up the symptoms of our problems may mitigate the worst of the current socioeconomic gaps and the most visible of the many forms of environmental degradation, but it does not overcome their root cause, it only treats the symptoms. Stop-gap measures do not change the thinking that gave rise to the problems we experience. We must find a better way to go. We cannot go back, and we cannot remain as we are. We must go forward.

Limiting CO_2 emissions, reducing income differentials, and safeguarding the quality of soil, air, and water are restitutive measures. They are important, but pursuing them is not doing something that is unconditionally good, only something that is less bad. In some cases, doing something less bad would not be good at all; it would extend the lifespan of the malfunctioning system and allow the problems engendered by it to intensify and become more intractable.

That doing something that is less bad is actually bad, seems like a paradox. But this is the case because the more we delay reaching the point where the current social, political, and economic system is sufficiently destabilized to be open to real change, the higher the cost of implementing the needed change becomes.

The global crisis in which we find ourselves is forcing us to change, and to change fundamentally. This is good, and even fortunate: crisis creates the opportunity to change. Deep crisis creates the opportunity to change our way of thinking. Among other things, it creates a higher level of solidarity among people and groups, the will to pull together. This has been the experience during WWII, when people threatened by Hitler's armies did not quibble or fight each other, but joined forces to face the danger they shared. Countless acts of solidarity and heroism were born. But do we have to wait for a further deepening crisis to come up with the solidarity to pull together?

We cannot afford to wait. Our "tried and tested" methods do not work, and trying to apply them may be a waste of time. Standard solutions do not work even in the economy and in the domain of technology. More and more economic growth and more and more sophisticated technologies are not the panacea they are believed to be. Economic growth, if not accompanied by the means and provisions of distributing its benefits, concentrates its payoffs on an ever smaller minority and exacerbates the gap between rich and poor. As the experience of recent years shows, a globalized economy focuses production, trade, finance, and communication in the hands of an ever smaller minority, and produces a backlash for the majority in the form of spreading unemployment, widening income gaps, and worsening environmental degradation. In this globalized economy, hundreds of millions are living at a higher material standard, but thousands of millions are pressed into abject poverty, subsisting in shantytowns and urban ghettos in the shadow of ostentatious affluence. The current forms of economic growth exclude an ever-growing segment of humanity and generate resentment, frustration, and violence.

In today's world, undifferentiated economic growth is both socially and politically explosive. It fuels resentment and revolt and provokes massive migration from the countryside to the cities, and from the poor to the affluent parts of the world. Under these conditions, organized crime — already a global enterprise — finds fertile ground; it engages in a whole gamut of activities, ranging from the control of information to prostitution, fake information, and traffic in arms, drugs, and human organs.

Technological advances without checks and balances in their application are likewise not the answer. Technology is a powerful tool, but it is a two-edged sword. Nuclear power offers a nearly unlimited supply of commercial energy, but the disposal of nuclear wastes and decommissioning aging reactors pose unsolved problems and constitute major threats. And the specter of nuclear meltdown remains on the horizon, whether it is due to technical accident or intentional terrorism.

Genetic engineering has a remarkable power to create bacteria-resistant and protein-rich plants, improved breeds of animals, vast supplies of animal proteins, and microorganisms that produce proteins and hormones and improve photosynthesis. But genetic engineering can also produce lethal biological weapons and pathogenic microorganisms, as well as abnormally aggressive animals and insects. Irresponsibly applied, genetic engineering reduces the diversity of species and harms the balance between populations in today's already destabilized ecologies.

Information technologies could create an interacting global community by linking people whatever their culture and ethnic or national origin, but the networks of communication, despite sophisticated preventive measures, remain open to violations of privacy and are prey to hackers. They remain open to illegitimate, illegal, and criminal uses, such as spy networks and arms trade. A growing number of information and communication networks are operating at the edge of legitimacy, serving underground interests such as sex, prostitution, pornography, and extortion.

What are we to do? If the usual prescriptions for addressing our problems no longer produce benefits, we have to replace them — we must create fundamental change in the system. The world we build needs to be sustainable and favorable to human existence and even human thriving; it cannot be a mere continuation of yesterday's world.

We already have noted that there is no way back; when we extrapolate current trends we do not get a sustainable world. We get a world that is not only prone to breakdown, but also is inevitably breaking down. Only the timing of its breakdown is uncertain.

In his March 1933 Inaugural Address, Franklin D. Roosevelt said that the only thing we have to fear is fear itself. This is wise advice. We are granted the chance to live up to it. We live at a time when we not only *need* to, but actually *can*, upshift up to a better world. This is not a time for fear; it is a time for action, for making our evolution consciously guided by our best intentions and deepest insights.

2. Forget In-Sane Beliefs

The second step to reform our evolution is remedial. It is to overcome the blockages that hinder us in guiding our evolution by our best intentions and deepest insights. This task begins with you. You need to take a good look at yourself. What values and beliefs do you pursue? What motivates your being in this world?

These questions merit an honest answer. Here are some pointers to search for such an answer.

Question Irrational Practices

In 2004, the Wisdom Council of the international think tank The Club of Budapest issued a declaration that questions a number of practices that hallmark the contemporary world. These practices are still widely followed, although they are paradoxical and even irrational. The Wisdom Council asked, *Where is the wisdom in a system that:*

- produces weapons that are more dangerous than the conflicts they are meant to solve?
- creates an overproduction of food, but fails to make it available to those who are hungry?
- allows half of the world's children to live in poverty and millions of them to suffer acute hunger?
- fails to appreciate and make use of the sensitivity, care, and sense of solidarity women bring to the family and the community, and could bring to politics and business?
- faces a gamut of tasks and challenges, yet puts more and more people out of work?
- gives full priority to maximizing the productivity of labor (even though millions are unemployed or underemployed) rather than improving the productivity of resources (notwithstanding that most natural resources are finite, and many are scarce and nonrenewable)?
- requires unrelenting economic and financial growth just to function and not to crash?
- faces long-term structural and operational problems, yet bases its criteria of success on three-month accounting periods and the day-to-day fluctuation of stock exchanges?

- assesses social and economic progress in terms of the gross national product and leaves out of account the quality of people's lives and how well their basic needs are fulfilled?
- fights religious fundamentalism but enshrines "market fundamentalism" (the belief that unrestrained competition on the market can right all wrongs and solve all problems)?
- expects people in their private sphere to abide by the golden rule "treat others as you expect others to treat you," yet ignores this elementary principle of fairness and equity in politics (to treat other states as you expect other states to treat your state) as well as in business (to treat partners and competitors as you expect partners and competitors to treat your business)?

Question Some Widespread Aspirations

- The Cult of Efficiency. *I must get the maximum out of every person, every machine, and every organization regardless of what is produced and whether or not it serves a useful purpose.*
  —Efficiency without regard to what is produced and whom it will benefit leads to mounting unemployment, catering to the demands of the rich without regard to the needs of the poor, and polarizes society into "monetized" and "traditional" sectors.

- The Technological Imperative. *Anything that can be done ought to be done. If it can be made or performed, it can be sold, and if it is sold, it is good for us and the economy.*
  —The technological imperative has resulted in a plethora of goods that people only think they need; some of them are not only unnecessary, but also actually harmful.

- The Newer Is the Better. *Anything that is new is better than (almost) anything that we had even last year.*
  —That the new would always be better is simply not true. Often, the new is worse than the "old" that it replaced: more expensive, more wasteful, more damaging to health, and more polluting, alienating, or stressful.

- Economic Rationality Is Paramount. *The value of everybody, including neighbors, partners, clients, and customers can be calculated in money. What I want is what everybody wants: to amass money. The rest is idle conversation and mere pretense.*
  —The reduction of everything and everybody to economic value may have seemed rational during epochs in which a great economic upswing turned all heads and pushed everything else into the background, but it is foolhardy at a time when people are beginning to rediscover deep-rooted social and spiritual values and to cultivate lifestyles of voluntary simplicity.

- My Country, Right or Wrong. *Come what may, I owe unwavering allegiance only to one flag and one government.*
  —The chauvinistic assertion "my country, right or wrong" has played untold havoc both domestically and internationally, calling for people to fight for causes a new government later repudiates, to espouse the values and worldviews of a small group of political leaders, and to ignore the growing cultural, social, and economic ties that evolve among people in different parts of the globe. Yet, there is nothing in the healthy human psychology that would forbid the expansion of loyalty above the level of the country one happened to have been born into. No individual needs to swear exclusive allegiance to one

flag only. We can be loyal to several segments of society without being disloyal to any. We can be loyal to our community without giving up loyalty to our province, state, or region. We can be loyal to our region and feel at one with an entire culture and with the human family as a whole. As Europeans are English, German, French, Spanish, and Italian as well as European, and as Americans are New Englanders, Texans, Southerners, and Pacific Northwesterners as well as American, so people in all parts of the world possess multiple identities and can develop multiple allegiances to them.

- The Future Is None of My Business. *Why should I worry about the interest of the next generation? Every generation has had to look after itself, and the present and the next generations will have to do the same.* —Living without conscious forward planning, although it may have been fine in days of rapid growth when each new generation could ensure a good life for itself, is not a responsible option at a time of global shift, when the rationality of the past is in question and the rationality that will decide the life and wellbeing of future generations is not yet in place. Yet, we already know that the decisions we make today will have a profound impact on the generations that come after us.

Discard Outdated Beliefs

- *The Environment Is an Inexhaustible Reservoir of Resources.* The assumption that, for all practical intents and purposes, the environment provided by the planet's biosphere is an infinite source of resources and an infinite sink of wastes.

This belief is persistent but misguided. Its origins go back to the archaic empires. It would hardly have occurred to the inhabitants of ancient Babylonia, Sumer, Egypt, India, or China that the world in which they lived could ever be exhausted of the basic necessities of life — edible plants, domestic animals, clean water, and breathable air — or fouled by dumping wastes and garbage in it. Nature appeared to be far too vast to be tainted, polluted, or defiled by what humans did in their settlements and on the lands that surround them.

The belief in an environment that is an inexhaustible fountain of the resources we want for our life gave rise to the faulty way our forebears have been relating to the natural environment for most of recorded history. It originated nearly ten thousand years ago in the Levant. Until then, indigenous communities in Africa, Asia, and pre-Colombian America had a deep respect for the environment and used only as much as nature could regenerate. From the time of the so-called Neolithic Revolution (which saw the beginning of humans domesticating plants and animals for their own purposes), some communities began not only to exploit but also to overexploit their environments. The Mycenaean and Olmec civilizations and those of the Indus Valley are notable examples. In the Fertile Crescent, this practice produced historical consequences. There, at the cradle of Western civilization, humans were not content with the perennial rhythms and cycles of nature, but sought ways to harness nature for their own ends. The land, though hot and arid in spots, appeared amenable to exploitation. Yet there were problems even in the friendly environments. In some places, such as ancient Sumer, flash floods washed away irrigation channels and dams and left fields arid.

The assumption that the resources provided by the environment are inexhaustible made much of the Fertile Crescent of biblical times into the Middle East of today — a region with vast areas of arid, infertile land. But people could move on, colonizing new lands and exploiting fresh resources.

In the Nile Valley, the environment was more benign. Great rivers irrigated the land, brought in silt, and washed away wastes. The archaic civilizations were mostly riverine civilizations built on the shores not only of the Nile but also of the Yellow River, the Tigris and Euphrates, the Ganges, and the Huang-Ho.

Today, when we overexploit our environments we have nowhere left to go. In a globally extended industrial civilization that wields powerful technologies, the belief in the inexhaustibility of nature is irrational and dangerous. It gives reign to the overuse and thoughtless impairment of the resources of the planet and to the overload of the biosphere's self-regenerative capacities. Persistence in practices inspired by the belief in the inexhaustibility of the planet's resources leads to an impoverished and inhospitable environment incapable of supplying the resources required by an enormous and still growing population.

- *Nature Is a Giant Mechanism.* Another assumption that is now obsolete dates from the early modern age, a consequence of the Newtonian view of the world. The idea of nature as a giant mechanism was adapted to medieval technologies such as watermills and windmills, pumps, mechanical clocks, and animal-drawn plows and carriages, but it fails when it comes to nuclear reactors, networked computers, and genetically engineered plants and microbes. Sophisticated technologies are not Newtonian machines, and they do not obey mechanical laws.

Yet the assumption that nature can be engineered like a machine has persisted to our day. The basic idea supporting this belief is that doing one thing can always be relied upon to lead to another thing — much as pressing a key on an old-fashioned typewriter always makes an arm lift and print the corresponding letter. On the modern computer, however, sophisticated programs interpret the information entered on the keyboard and decide the outcome.

The mechanistic concept works even less well when man-made technologies are interfaced with natural processes. The way a transplanted gene is expressed in a given species of plant is foreseeable for that plant, but it is not foreseeable when it comes to the interaction of that plant with other plants in its environment. The same gene that produces the foreseen and desired effect in the transgenic plant can produce unforeseen and undesirable effects in other species.

A "horizontal gene-transfer" is always a possibility, but its long-term consequences for the ecosystem are unpredictable. Such consequences have already proved disastrous for the integrity of nature and the productivity of agricultural lands in Asia, Africa, and Latin America.

Nonetheless, pre-pandemic industrial civilization persisted in treating both its technologies and its natural environment as mechanisms that can be engineered and reengineered. The result has been the progressive degradation of water, air, and soil, and the impairment of local and continental ecosystems.

- *Life Is a Struggle Where Only the Fit Survive.* Yet another obsolete assumption dates from the nineteenth century. It is an entailment of Darwin's theory of natural selection. It claims that in society, as in nature, only the fit survive. This means that if we want to survive, we have to be fit — in fact fitter than our competitors — for the existential struggle.

As is discussed in Information Note (4) of this book, current evolutionary science has unequivocally overturned this outdated view with new understandings of the overriding role of cooperation in evolution and a clear understanding of how altruism — goodness itself — actually evolves. Regarding cultural evolution, current science, as this guide explains later, now also points toward a planetary altruism, or in the words of a "motto" of the United Nations' Sustainable Development Goals: "a world that works for all." In the context of society, of course, fitness is not determined by the genes but includes cultural traits such as smartness, daring, ambition, and the will to pursue our ends without being blocked by the anticipation of their unintended consequences.

Transposing nineteenth-century Darwinism into the sphere of society is dangerous, as the "social Darwinism" of the Nazi ideology demonstrated. Hitler's regime justified the conquest of territories in the name of acquiring adequate *Lebensraum* (living space) and warranted the subjugation of other peoples in the name of racial fitness.

In our day, the consequences of social Darwinism have gone beyond armed aggression to the less evident but in some ways equally damaging merciless struggle of competitors in the marketplace. All-out competition has produced widening gaps between rich and poor and concentrated wealth and power in the hands of the winners: corporate managers and international financiers. States and entire populations have been relegated to the role of clients and consumers and, if poor and powerless, have been dismissed as marginal factors in the equations that determine success in the marketplace. However, as is reported in Information Note (4), the foundations of Social Darwinism are now definitely rejected in science. Yet, many people in modern societies continue to uphold this obsolete concept.

- *The Market Distributes the Benefits.* For most of the late twentieth and early twenty-first centuries, the financial community operated on the assumption that, as the economists' doctrine maintains, "the market ensures optimal capital allocation through the efficient incorporation of all available and relevant information into share prices."

  This assumption is still shared by most business people. It is a counterpart of the assumption that life is a struggle where the fittest survive. Unlike in nature — where insufficient fitness results in the extinction of the species — in society, there is the market, a mechanism that distributes benefits and, thus, counteracts the processes of natural selection. The market is governed by what Adam Smith called the "invisible hand." It assures those who do well for themselves that they do well also for others. Wealth trickles down from the rich to the poor.

  Belief in the invisible hand of the market is comforting, and this doctrine is often cited by the winners to avert reproach for not caring for the losers. Unfortunately, the doctrine of the free market leaves out of account the fact that markets are not entirely free. Yet it would distribute benefits only under conditions of perfect or near-perfect competition. There has never been perfect or even near-perfect competition in the world — the playing field is never level. Inevitably, it is distorted in favor of the winners and to the detriment of the losers. This produces the kind of skewed income distribution we have in the world: the poorest 40 percent have 3 percent of the global wealth, and the wealth of a few hundred billionaires equals the income of half of the world's population.

- *The More You Consume the Better You Are.* This is the assumption that there is a correspondence between the size of your wallet and your personal worth as the owner of the wallet.

  The equivalence of human worth with financial worth has been consciously fueled by the business community. Some companies covertly, if no longer openly, maintain that consumption itself is the ideal. After WWII, Victor Lebov, a U.S. retailing analyst, put forward the consumerist philosophy in clear language. "Our enormously productive economy," he wrote, "demands that we make consumption our way of life, that we convert the buying and use of goods into rituals, that we seek our spiritual satisfaction, our ego satisfaction, in consumption. The economy needs things consumed, burned, worn out, replaced, and discarded at an ever-increasing rate." Such unashamed promulgation of unlimited consumption cannot be maintained today, but it can be implied. It is implied in advertising consumption that harms the world, and harms in the last count the consumer in the world.

  The belief that consumption is good for the consumer and good for the economy has been a powerful engine of growth in the economy. This engine ignored and failed to take into account the fact that ever more people consuming ever more resources is not sustainable in a finite world. It leads to the inequities, resentments, and stresses we have experienced in recent years.

- *Achieving Economic Ends Justifies Military Means.* The ancient Romans had a saying: if you aspire to peace, prepare for war. They aspired for peace and were ready for war. The Romans had a worldwide empire, with rebellious peoples within and barbarian tribes at the periphery. Maintaining it required a constant exercise of military power. The belief in using military means to achieve political and economic ends persists in the modern world. Most people hold that if our national independence and economic goals are threatened, we have good reason to "call in the Marines."

  As the wars fought for the control first of coal and then oil demonstrated, recourse to armed intervention was considered legitimate when economic and territorial interests required it. Yet this belief is counter-functional in a world where local conflicts can escalate to global confrontation, and the parties to the conflict have access to weapons that can harm and destroy not just the presumed enemy, but also all parties to the conflict. Using military means to achieve economic ends is a high-risk and entirely in-sane option in the twenty-first century.

Rethink Even Long-Standing Convictions

In addition to the beliefs and assumptions we have just reviewed, a number of widespread convictions are badly in need of being abandoned. Here are a few:

- *Everything Is Reversible.* The current crisis, as other epidemics and crises before it, is but a temporary perturbation after which everything goes back to normal. All we need to do is manage the problems with tried and tested methods. Business-as-unusual has evolved out of business-as-usual, and sooner or later it will reverse back into it.

- *Everyone Is Unique and Separate.* We are all unique and separate individuals enclosed in our skin and pursuing our own interests. The same as our country, we have only ourselves to rely on; everyone else is either friend or foe, at best linked to us by ties of mutual — even if provisional and temporary — interest.

- *Order Calls for Hierarchy.* Order in society can only be achieved by rules and laws and their proper enforcement, and this requires a chain of command recognized and obeyed by all. A few people on top (usually males) make up the rules, legislate the laws, give the orders, and ensure compliance with them. Everyone else is to obey the rules and take his or her place within the political hierarchy.

- *The Ideology of Westphalia.* The legal conventions coming into force at the end of WWI with the Peace of Westphalia conferred on nation-states the "inalienable right" to have an independent government, internationally recognized boundaries, a national currency and a national army, diplomatic relations with other states, and action free from fetters within their own borders. The formally constituted nation-state became the sole political authority, the only entity possessing legal and political sovereignty.

These convictions are steering us the wrong way.

- No experience of shocks and crises will change our values and behaviors if we remain convinced that the problems we encounter are temporary disturbances in an unchanging and perhaps unchangeable status quo.

- Seeing ourselves as separate from the rest of the world could convert natural impulses to seek our own advantage into a win-lose struggle to achieve our own aims regardless of the cost to others. This is a shortsighted strategy to follow for individuals as well as for states and businesses.

- Male-dominated hierarchies have worked in the army and also in the organized church, but they have not proven effective in business and in education. Successful managers and wise deans have learned the advantages of cooperative structures, but social and political institutions have continued to operate in a hierarchical mode. As a result, both state administrations and schools and universities have tended to be slow, their workings cumbersome and inefficient.

- We do not need to discard the idea of nation-state and the global system based on nation-states — it is a great advance over autocratic and hierarchical kingdoms, princedoms, and feudal regimes. But the nation-state is not independent of other social and political systems: it is not sovereign. It is not the only or even the principal form of organization of human life and, thus, not the only form that deserves our allegiance. The nation-state is but one level of organization in the system of human life on the planet. All societies are elements of organized human life in the great scheme which is "Gaia" — the system of life on the planet. It is that system that deserves our highest allegiance and deepest devotion, and not the nation-state.

The re-assignment of our allegiance to the system of life on the planet is in our own interest: it is the best and most assured way to ensure our persisting and thriving on Earth.

Question Some Cherished Aspirations

If we are not to fall back into the inequitable, dangerous, and downright irrational practices that hold sway in the world, we need to review and adapt our aspirations.

You can start by focusing on the paramount task of looking for, and actively seeking, a balance between needs and resources. This balance has not been achieved in recent years, and it will not be achieved until there is a fundamental change in the way people manage the resources they need.

The current distribution of the resources generated by economic activity is unfair and unsustainable. The rich are still getting richer, and the poor, poorer. The population of the poor has been growing faster than the population of the relatively affluent. If this trend were to continue, by the middle of this century, over 90 percent of the more than 9 billion people who will then live on earth would live in poverty.

When it comes to resource use, the issue is not numbers, but quality. It is not how *many* people use the planet's resources, but *how well* they use them. Our world has enough, as Gandhi said, to provide for all people's *need*, but not enough to provide even for one man's *greed.*

In the industrialized parts of the world, greed is dominant. In the name of freedom and laissez-faire capitalism, irresponsible values and beliefs give reign to selfishness and ostentation. Living by the dominant values and aspirations entails an excessive consumption of nonrenewable resources and an excessive production of waste. Those who "enjoy" the modern world's living standard use 80 percent of the world's energy and raw materials and contribute the lion's share of its pollution.

Irresponsibility and greed show up also in people's eating habits. The affluent consume an unsustainable amount of processed foods and expensive items such as red meat. The planet's entire grain harvest would not be enough to feed the cattle that would be needed if all people in the world would adopt such eating habits.

Those who can afford it use a disproportionate share of commercial energy as well. They heat their homes with inefficient gas-powered heaters or electric radiators and leave air conditioners running all day. Until recently, they were driving gas-guzzling vans, pick-up trucks, and sport utility vehicles, in preferences to hybrids and electric vehicles.

It merits remarking that, even though the affluent are using an excessive share of the planet's resources, they do not achieve by that a better quality of life. The modern ideal of luxury is flawed. The advertising world's paradigm of luxury — lounging by the pool, smoking a cigarette, sipping a daiquiri, munching on a hamburger, and talking on the cell phone — backfires. This lifestyle is neither healthy nor satisfying. It can lead to a number of chronic diseases, including skin cancer, lung cancer, cirrhosis of the liver, high cholesterol, and brain damage. In the last count, leading a life of luxury is not much of an improvement over working in a high-pressure job, taking smoke breaks every hour, having a drink after work to relax, and falling asleep in front of the television.

There are better ways to live. There are meaningful and important tasks we can achieve whatever our lot in life. There are scores of healthy and rewarding ways to spend one's leisure time. Helping neighbors, creating a better community, visiting sites of natural, historical, or cultural interest, hiking, swimming, biking, reading, listening to music, or taking an interest in literature and culture are satisfying pursuits that do not involve a high level of material and energy consumption and do not require a great deal of money. They are healthier for you and easier on the environment than striving to satisfy the mainstream ideal of luxury.

Better aspirations would give rise to behaviors that free a significant portion of the planet's resources for human consumption. For example, it takes 190 square meters of land and 105,000 liters of water to produce one kilogram of grain-fed feedlot beef, but to produce one kilogram of soybeans takes only 16 square meters of land and 9,000 liters of water. On the same amount of land where farmers catering to the preferences of the rich have been producing one kilogram of beef, they could produce almost 12 kilograms of soybeans or 8.6 kilograms of corn. It would save 96,000 liters of water to choose soybeans and 92,500 liters of water to choose planting corn.

Eating fresh produce, living closer to nature, using public transportation, and walking on foot instead of sitting in cars are healthier than eating red meat and junk food, and sitting in cars in overcrowded cities and jammed highways. Given the rapid erosion of agricultural lands and the threatening water squeeze, adopting more responsive aspirations on the part of a critical mass is essential for the health of the planet, as well as for the health of people on the planet.

The responsible kind of aspirations are guided by a morality that is fair for all. The applicable principle is that what is truly moral, is that which is good for everyone. Acting on this principle is rare in the modern world, but not in traditional societies. The great religions have been effective in setting the norms of morality, and they recognized the need for fairness in all things, including the distribution of resources. The Ten Commandments of Jews and Christians, the provisions for the faithful in Islam, and the Rules of Right Livelihood of the Buddhists are examples. But in recent times, the rise of science reduced the power of religious injunctions to regulate social behavior. Scientists, with some notable exceptions, did not come up with principles that would provide a basis for a universally acceptable moral code. Saint-Simon in the late 1700s, Auguste Comte in the early 1800s, and Émile Durkheim in the late 1800s and early 1900s tried to develop a "positive" scientific observation- and experiment-based ethic, but their initiatives conflicted with the science community's commitment to value neutrality. It was not picked up by the mainstream in society.

In the late twentieth century, ever more scientists joined spiritual leaders in recognizing the need for principles that suggest a universal code for moral behavior. The Union of Concerned Scientists, an organization of leading scientists, issued a statement in 1993 signed by 1,670 scientists from seventy countries including more than a hundred Nobel laureates. The ethic we need, said the scientists, "must motivate a great movement convincing reluctant leaders and reluctant governments and reluctant peoples themselves to effect the needed changes." The signatories noted the human responsibility for caring for the planet and warned that "a great change in our stewardship of the Earth and the life on it is required if vast human misery is to be avoided and our global home … is not to be irretrievably mutilated."

In the last few decades, vast human misery has not been avoided, and we are not sure whether or not our global home has already been irretrievably mutilated. In any event, we need a trustworthy and fair moral code that takes into account everyone's wellbeing, not only that of the rich and the powerful.

3. Value Diversity

Updating your obsolete beliefs and assumptions and reviewing and perhaps reconsidering your aspirations are essential steps to take, and there are also others. We must all learn not just to tolerate but to actually *value* diversity.

You need to allow for the emergence of cultures, some of which are very different from yours, on the contemporary stage.

Living in harmony with different peoples is a challenge. They think differently, possess different values and ideals, and have different lifeways. Yet you must live in harmony with them if this planet is not to be an arena of growing conflicts and catastrophic breakdowns.

The difficulty of living in harmony with other peoples and cultures is not to be underestimated. Most people in the Western world think that everybody is like them and wants to live like them. They think everybody wants the same thing: money, power, sex, and to have a good time. Claiming otherwise, they believe, is but sophistry and pretense.

This belief does not check with reality. While it is true that the values of Western technological society shape most people's behavior, a great deal of diversity remains underneath. There is diversity in the way people view themselves, their society and nature, and conceive of liberty and justice. Disregarding, or even underestimating, the diversity of the cultures of the world has produced disastrous consequences in the past. It produced conflict escalating into bloodbaths in the Balkans, Ireland, the Middle East, the Arab world, sub-Saharan Africa, Latin America, the Indian subcontinent, as well as in Southeast Asia. Even international terrorism, as distinct from aggression and violence due to current or inherited prejudice and intolerance, has a cultural basis. It is fed by intense hatred, resentment, and the desire for vengeance.

Whether in the Balkans, in the Middle East, or elsewhere in the world, there is a need for better understanding cultural differences among people and societies. The spread of the internet, of MacDonaldism, of Coca-Colonization, and of modern consumer culture did not eliminate cultural diversity — it only masks it. Underneath the surface, the diversity of human societies remains real and powerful, even if somewhat reduced.

4. Curate Hopeful Monsters

There is a term used by cultural anthropologists that is particularly applicable today: "hopeful monster." A hopeful monster is one who is further along the path of evolution than the mainstream, and does not fit the mainstream's idea of what is normal and right. In the eyes of the bulk of the population, they are "monsters." But we know that they are "hopeful" monsters because as evolution unfolds around them, they will be recognized not just as belonging to the mainstream, but as pioneers of a new mainstream.

There are a number of hopeful monsters today among the cultures that arise at the periphery of the cultural landscape. To look for and understand them, we have to clarify what we mean by "culture." According to a simple but applicable definition, a culture is the ensemble of the values, worldviews, and aspirations that characterize a group of people and distinguish it from others. Contemporary societies have their own cultures, and their cultures are not monolithic. There is usually a dominant culture at the center and a number of alternative cultures on the periphery.

There is a culture at the periphery that qualifies to be called hopeful monster. It is made up of people who are rethinking their preferences, priorities, values, and behaviors, and are ready to shift from the ideal of consumption based on quantity toward quality defined by environmental friendliness, sustainability, and the ethics of production and use. They seek to, and in some instances already do, replace matter- and energy-wasteful technologies and practices with lifestyles hallmarked by voluntary simplicity and the search for coherence with people and nature. As this nascent culture moves toward the center, those who embrace it bypass the negative characteristics of New Age cultures, such as antisocial activities, promiscuous sex, and isolation. They are united by the ideal of living in harmony with nature, and reject the artificial impersonality of the mainstream culture. A better culture is being born, and it could grow.

California's Institute of Noetic Sciences (IONS) [see Catalog of Upshifting Organizations] summed up the shifts that make for the birth of a hopeful monster.

- *The Shift from Competition to Reconciliation and Partnership*: a change from relationships, organizational models, and societal strategies based on competition to relationships and models based on principles of healing, reconciliation, forgiveness, and male–female partnership.

- *The Shift from Greed and Scarcity to Sufficiency and Caring*: a change in values, perspectives, and approaches from the traditional self-centered and greedy mode toward a sense of the sufficient and the interpersonal concern of caring.

- *The Shift from Outer to Inner Authority*: a change from reliance on outer sources of "authority" to inner sources of "knowing."

- *The Shift from Separation to Wholeness*: a recognition of the wholeness and interconnectedness of all aspects of reality.

- *The Shift from Mechanistic to Living Systems*: a shift of attention from models of organizations based on mechanistic systems to perspectives and approaches rooted in the principles that inform the world of the living.

- *The Shift from Organizational Fragmentation to Coherent Integration*: a shift from disintegrative, fragmented organizations with parts set against each other to goals and structures integrated, so they serve both those who participate in the organizations and those around them.

A rapid shift of the hopeful monsters toward the center may seem optimistic; in ordinary circumstances, it would be utopian. But we live in non-ordinary times. The crises we experience create instability at the center, and this allows the hopeful monsters at the periphery to grow in numbers and in influence. Butterfly effects surface — minute fluctuations trigger major storms. This means that even small groups of people can create major change.

There are many ways we can support the ascent of the hopeful monsters toward the center. We can take one or another of the following ways.

The Way Through Self-Exploration

People who practice meditation or engage in intense prayer can contribute to the needed culture shift by exploring their own intuitions, values, and motivations. They find elements in the deep dimension of their consciousness that invite them toward harmony with people and planet. Astronauts who had the privilege of traveling in space and viewing Earth in its living splendor discovered these elements in their own psyche. The intense tie they experienced to their planetary home changed their life, and it seems to persist for the rest of their life.

Not only astronauts who could behold our planet from outer space, but also ordinary people here on earth can experience our oneness with the planet. There are various notable experiences that produce this shift in your consciousness — the experience known as the NDE (near-death experience) is a prime example. People who return from the portals of death see themselves and the world in a new light. They have a fresh appreciation of life and a deep reverence for nature. They develop humanitarian and ecological concerns. They realize that we cannot do anything to others without doing it to ourselves.

Evidently, not everyone can be expected to engage in deep meditation, travel in space, or have near-death experiences. Yet everyone can contribute to this shift because, as psychiatrist Stanislav Grof pointed out, everyone can enter altered states of consciousness. In these states, we experience space- and time-transcending ties to other people, and to the world around us. Grof noted that he has yet to meet a single person, no matter what his or her educational background, IQ, and profession, who would have had altered-state experiences and continued to subscribe to the fragmented materialist view of the world.

The Way Through the Aesthetic Experience

Self-exploration through altered states of consciousness is not the only way you can promote the advance of a hopeful monster. The experience of beauty and significance is another way. This is an experience that can be catalyzed by nature, as well as by human artifacts.

The beneficial effects of contact with nature have been well known to traditional cultures. They are rediscovered and activated today under the label of "nature therapy." In Japan, for example, many people practice "forest bathing": *Shin-rin yoku*. Forest bathing calls for going into a forest and feeling yourself become one with it — hearing the wind rustle through the leaves, sensing the play of light on the surface of a pond, feeling yourself floating with the clouds in the sky. Even to be in a forest proves healing. The sounds of nature sooth the nerves and calm the spirit.

The healing power of the nature experience is enhanced by direct bodily contact. This means embracing the trunk of a tree, or walking barefoot on unpaved ground. Such contact intensifies the experience and makes one *feel* the world. It encourages the insight that we are in everything, and everything is in us.

The experience of beauty and significance can be catalyzed by human artifacts as well. Philosophers and psychologists call this the "aesthetic experience." In moments of inspiration, painters, poets, musicians, writers, and other visionary and creative individuals experience oneness, solidarity, and a deep love for all things. The artifacts they create express this experience and catalyze it in others. Regardless of the particular mode in which the aesthetic experience is expressed, it connects the experiencer with people, with nature, and with the world at large. It lends credence to our intuitions of belonging to something larger than ourselves — to something sacred. According to psychologist William James, the experience of belonging is also conveyed by intense prayer, and contemporary psychotherapists find that it is likewise conveyed by the practice of mindfulness and meditation.

The experience of beauty and significance that is catalyzed by nature as well as by artifacts is not difficult to achieve. The aesthetic experiences are not limited to forests and mountains, or to museums, galleries, and concert halls. In one form or another, art is present throughout the human world. It shapes cities through architecture and urban design, enters our feelings through music and dance, and conveys deep insight through literature. No matter in what form they are expressed, experiences of oneness are powerful ways of curating the rise of the emerging cultures.

The Way Through Science

Innovations in science — unless they have immediate technological, economic, or social applications — are not immediately known by a wide layer of the population. Scientists use esoteric language and complex mathematics; their treatises are neither accessible nor understandable beyond their disciplinary fields. The result is that the general public is poorly informed about the latest revolutionary advances of scientific research. This fails to exploit an important resource for recovering the timeless insights of the human mind.

There are scientists and science-minded thinkers who are aware of the importance of filling the communications gap and have formulated insights coming to light in the sciences in everyday terms. Paul Davies, Deepak Chopra, Bruce Lipton, Gary Zukav, and Gregg Braden are among those who have contributed to the dissemination of key scientific insights to a wide public. They have written popular science books and held widely accessible lectures and podcasts on current advances in science. As evolutionary biologists David Sloan Wilson and Kurt Johnson wrote in a book subtitled *Evolutionary Visions and Hope for the Future*, mainstream science's evolutionary views are slowly "catching up" with the avant-garde visions. The process is slow, but seems inexorable. Physicist Roger Penrose finally received the Nobel Prize in 2020 for the pioneering work he published in 1965.[7]

Science, it appears, is evolving toward a holistic understanding of who we are, and what the world is. The classical ideas of Newton, Darwin, and Freud have been overtaken by new discoveries. In light of the contemporary sciences, matter, life, and mind are consistent elements within an overall system of great complexity yet coherent and harmonious design. The biosphere is born within the womb of the universe, and mind and consciousness are born in the womb of the biosphere. Nothing is independent of any other thing. Our bodies are part of the biosphere, and they resonate with the web of life on this planet. Our minds are part of our bodies, and they are in touch with other minds near and far.

The real world is not limited to what we perceive with our senses. In extends beyond the here and now. Whatever happens here also happens throughout space and time, and whatever happens in this moment has grown out of what has happened at times past and is the womb of what will happen in the future.

Looking into your own deeper self, and rising to the aesthetic experience, testify to our ties to each other to the world around us. These ties are confirmed by cutting-edge science. They are a hallmark both of intuitive, spontaneous hopeful monsters, as well as of those that are intellectually oriented. If we allow evolution to unfold on this planet, today's hopeful monsters will be part of mainstream tomorrow.

Information Note (3): A Pocket Atlas of Cultural Diversity and the New Ten Commandments

Here we offer a brief overview of the cultural diversity in today's world — the diversity that we must not just tolerate, but consciously value and further.

- In the southern half of the Americas, an aggressive brand of cultural nationalism has been emerging. Latin Americans resent their dependence on North America and resent being receivers rather than producers of the culture that shapes their societies. As part of their cultural heritage, they have a deep inherent spirituality that contrasts with the pragmatism of the culture of the United States.

- There are transcendentalist elements of the indigenous Latin American culture that date back to the fifteenth century. The Catholic scholasticism of the European Middle Ages was not merely a monastic philosophy — it was a spiritual system that governed every aspect of life. Subservience to ecclesiastical authority, like subservience to God and king, became axiomatic in everyday morality. Even when the colonial epoch drew to a close, there was no accommodation in Latin America between the scholastic legacy and Anglo-Saxon pragmatism. The businesslike mentality of the Anglo-Saxon world has never taken hold in the Southern part of the American continent.

- Western cultural domination is an agonizing issue for Arabs; they perceive it as an element of industrialized-country hegemony penetrating their countries. The Arab countries find themselves at the passive end of a dialogue that links them mainly with the culture of Western Europe and North America. The militant fundamentalism that has been emerging in the Arab world has been an expression of the resentment felt by Arab politicians, business leaders, and intellectuals in regard to the foreign domination emerging in this dialogue. In the Muslim culture as a whole, transcendentalism has been combined with monotheism, and in Sufism, it acquired a mystical streak.

- Mysticism also has been prevalent in the indigenous cultures of black Africa. These cultures have always been spiritualistic and animistic, and these features have not been eliminated in the traditional sectors of the population by the zeal of Christian missionaries, nor have they been overcome by the marketing propaganda of transnational corporations.

- India and the countries of South Asia have had prolonged contact with British culture, but despite their admiration and assimilation of many of its traits, they are intent on protecting their own millennia-old cultural heritage as shown by their deep admiration for Gandhi, Aurobindo, and their numerous spiritual leaders.

- Admiration mixed with fear has been a hallmark of the cultures of the young nations of sub-Saharan Africa. Though avid consumers of industrial culture, African leaders have been intent on fortifying the native cultural heritage. While the poor segment of the population remains steeped in traditional beliefs and ways of life, a small — and lately shrinking — elite of intellectuals has been searching for the roots of African identity and seeking the political power to reinforce it.

- Though in a different form, transcendentalism is also a feature of the Hindu and Buddhist cultures of the Indian subcontinent. It focuses people's attention on spiritual matters and functions as a counterweight to the rising materialism and consumerism of the "modernized" sector.

- The Eastern mind has conserved many aspects of its cultural heritage. The great cultural circle that radiated from China during the past millennium was shaped by the naturalism of Lao Tzu, the social discipline of Confucius, and the Buddha's quest for personal enlightenment. In the twentieth century, these cultural origins branched in different directions, giving rise to the orthodox culture of Mao's Yan'an, the pragmatic culture of Hong Kong's Kong-Tai, and the mix of naturalism, Confucianism, and Buddhism that still characterizes the culture of Japan. Asian cultures became "modernized" but not Westernized. Eastern work habits, group loyalties, and lifestyles have remained culture-specific and different from those of Europe and North America.

- In modern-day Russia, historical experience has made for a profound ambivalence regarding Western culture. There is persistent admiration for the achievements of the West in technology as well as in high culture, but there is also a persistent demand to ensure that foreign influences do not overwhelm Russia's own cultural heritage.

- On the European continent, the same as in North America, materialistic individualism and pragmatism are still dominant, but they are not uniform and not monolithic. They are laced with a rising appreciation, although we share the same continent, but we have not become the same ourselves.

- New elements have been added today to the diversity of the contemporary world; elements that heighten, and not flatten, diversity. Now we not only share the modern consumer culture with its shopping malls and multiple enticements, not only get on the same internet, watch the same programs on television, eat the same foods and dress in the same ways, we also face common threats to our health, experience common suffering from extreme weather, are exposed to the trauma of war, and experience increasing uncertainties in regard to our jobs and means of livelihood. Faced with these issues, people do not all respond in the same way: they respond in light of their values and worldview. Contemporary peoples are diverse crews in the same boat. Their boats are becoming increasingly the same, but the crews themselves less so.

The New Ten Commandments

1. Live in ways that meet your needs and allow you to pursue your objectives without detracting from the chances of other people to meet their needs and pursue their objectives.

2. Live in ways that respect the right to life and to economic and cultural development of all people, wherever they live and whatever their ethnic origin, sex, citizenship, station in life, and belief system.

3. Live in ways that safeguard the right to live in a viable environment of all the living things that inhabit the earth.

4. Pursue happiness, freedom, and personal fulfillment in harmony with the integrity of nature and with consideration of the related pursuits of others around you.

5. Require of your political leaders that they relate to other peoples peacefully and in a spirit of cooperation, recognizing the legitimate aspirations for a better life and a healthy environment of all members of the human family.

6. Require of your business leaders that they accept responsibility not only for the owners and shareholders of their enterprises, but also for all its stakeholders. They are to produce goods and offer services that satisfy all legitimate demand without impairing nature and reducing the opportunities of small enterprises and poor economies to compete in the marketplace.

7. Require public media to provide a constant stream of reliable information on basic trends and crucial processes in order to enable people to reach informed decisions on issues that affect their health, prosperity, and future.

8. Make room in your life to help those less privileged than yourself to live a life of dignity, free from the struggles and humiliations of abject poverty.

9. Work with like-minded people to preserve or restore the essential balances of the environment in your neighborhood, and if you can, in other parts of the world as well.

10. Encourage young people and open-minded people of all ages to evolve the spirit that could empower them to make ethical decisions on issues that decide their future, and the future of their families, friends, and children.

CHAPTER 6

BE THE CHANGE YOU WANT TO SEE IN THE WORLD

Evolution in nature, we said, is impelled and guided by a holotropic attractor. This is confirmed by observation: living systems manifest a tendency among their parts and elements toward wholeness and coherence. We must assume that there is a force or factor in nature responsible for this tendency, as the known laws of nature alone do not fulfill this requirement.

However, evolution, as we noted, is nonlinear: it unfolds through recurring fallbacks and forward leaps. Crisis and incoherence make up the bulk of today's everyday experience, but this is due to a temporary and basically superficial fluctuation. Below the surface, there is an ongoing progression toward connection and coherence. Notwithstanding the fluctuations, evolution creates complex and connected systems — systems that are coherent in themselves and are coherently related to the world around them.

We are part of the evolution that unfolds on this planet, and we are not passive subjects of the unfolding of evolution; we are conscious beings who can act to make their evolution conscious and orient themselves according to their conscious insights. We have a sensitive brain and nervous system, and a uniquely articulate view of the world. Regrettably, we have not been using them to best advantage. We allowed selfishness and narrow horizons to dominate the world. They produced chaos and conflict, fed by intolerance and violence. We need to change the world, and for that, we need to change ourselves.

Gandhi's saying is the key. We must *be* the change we want to see in the world. How to be that change is the question. Here are some guiding principles.

1. Evolve Your Consciousness

Creating conscious evolution for humanity calls for evolving your consciousness. The shift we need is from fragmented and fragmenting, to holistic and wholeness-promoting consciousness. Evolution in nature and the universe drives toward wholeness, and human consciousness needs to reflect this evolutionary drive. We need to think in terms of wholes — of coherent and integral entities that maintain themselves and respond to the challenges of their environment.

The holistic view of the world is a basic element of the consciousness we need to evolve in the world. The fragmented, mechanistic mindset supports self-promoting, fragmented aspirations and actions. It already has broken apart the integrity of the social, economic, and political systems of the world. Humanity, the same as other systems of life on Earth, is healthy when it is whole, and sick when it is fragmented. We cannot reduce a whole system to its parts without losing the very element that makes it whole. This must be rectified: we need a planetary cure — a consciousness revolution.

The sciences of life are clear regarding the wholeness of life. The web of life on the planet cannot be dissembled into separate parts without creating decay and decomposition. Life is one, and when it is cared for as one, it thrives. We are healthy when we are whole, and life on the planet is healthy when it is whole. Intuitively we have known this, but we have buried this insight under a stressful and ever more desperate scramble for short-term selfish ends, seeking money and power, above all.

We have developed amazing energy and information technologies but applied them single-mindedly to achieve our immediate ends without regard for the consequences for others and for nature. We have made our technologies respond to our superficial wants, but allowed them to neglect our real needs. We have created an unsustainable world, prone to crisis and breakdown.

We need to adopt a holistic consciousness. Given the opportunity conferred by the current crisis, we can live up to this requirement. You, a conscious and purposive member of the human community, need to evolve a consciousness that enables you to see yourself as an intrinsic part of the evolution that unfolds in nature and the universe.

A holistic consciousness has been a standard feature of the mindset of traditional cultures. Traditional people did not intellectually know, but they intrinsically *felt*, that what is good for them individually is good for their community. In modern societies, this insight has been abandoned. Business and political leaders extol the individual and serve single-mindedly his interests. The operative principle in contemporary society is contrary to the holistic principle: what is good for the part is tacitly assumed to be good for the whole. Political and business leaders pursue the good of their own country or company with, at best, a pious hope that it may prove to be good for the rest.

The unholy principle is the ideology of individual nation- or enterprise-centered politics. It came to the fore in the U.S. congressional testimony of Charlie Wilson, then president of General Motors. Speaking at a congressional hearing, he said, "What is good for General Motors is good for the country." Few people have been contesting this philosophy. Even John F. Kennedy said that "a rising tide lifts all boats." We should add that a rising tide does *not* lift a strongly leaking boat.

That the immediate interests of the individual do not necessarily translate into the interests of the community in which that individual is embedded holds true for entire states and nations. Putting "America first" is a shortsighted policy when practiced as the Trump administration practiced it. It motivated the withdrawal of the U.S. from the Paris Accord on Climate Change, and prompted stopping support for international bodies such as UNESCO and the World Health Organization.

The same unholy philosophy was behind Hitler's proclamation, *Deutschland uber Alles* ("Germany above all"). It sought to legitimize Germany's invasion of Poland, annexation of Austria, and the world-domination ambitions of the Nazi regime. More recently, the same principle has been used to legitimate in the eyes of the Russian people Putin's decision to invade Ukraine.

Sooner or later, the unholy principle produces a backlash. At the end of WWII, it created disastrous conditions for Germany, and had it been pursued by the U.S. administration, it would have produced disastrous consequences for America. It is producing disastrous consequences for Russia itself.

2. Upgrade Your Spirituality

Aristotle said that we are social beings, and modern consciousness research confirms this. It affirms that we are not only social but also *spiritual* beings. Spirituality is not something some people are born with and others not. It is an intrinsic attribute of all human beings.

The problem is that, although we are spiritual in essence, only a few of us are spiritual in behavior. Our spirituality needs to be deepened to become effective. Gandhi was a deeply spiritual person himself. He knew what he was talking about when he advised that to create change in the world, we must ourselves become that change.

We need to unblock our inborn spirituality, free it from the layers of prejudice that accumulated around the meaning of spirituality. Spirituality is viewed by today's matter-of-fact individuals as a kind of idealistic adventuring; spiritual tenets are but imagination, wishful thinking at best.

Spirituality has been around for thousands of years, and the insights it conveys have been examined and tested by hundreds of different cultures. These insights hold water. And today, they are needed to counterbalance the narrow pragmatism that dominates the world.

How do you become a more spiritual person? The self-taught spiritual master Pierre Pradervand suggests that you begin by asking yourself two questions:

1) *What is my true priority in life? What am I really seeking?*
   Finding personal serenity? Helping to build a win-win world that works for all? Preparing the next reincarnation? Getting ahead in life, socially and materially?

2) *What is the real motivation of my spiritual search?*
   Finding inner peace? Expressing unconditional love? A life of service? The elevation of the collective level of consciousness? Or just my own enlightenment?

You need to reconnect with nature, life, and the universe, and spirituality helps you to *experience* these connections. It helps you to experience yourself as a being who seeks oneness with other beings, nature and the universe.

Repeated experiments show that the kind of spontaneous insight that speaks to our oneness does not appear at the ordinary frequencies of the waves emitted by our brain — of the EEG (electroencephalograph) spectrum. As a rule, deeper insight surfaces to waking consciousness below the frequency range of sense-perceivable reality: it surfaces in the Alpha domain, and even below, in the Theta and Delta range. Spiritual people are more likely to resonate with deep insight than purely rational individuals. The latter seldom perceive the dimension of the world below the Beta level.

The conclusion may appear surprising, but it is well-founded: there is a true need for spirituality in today's world. Becoming more spiritual is an essential condition of becoming a person whose being could transform the evolution of humankind on the planet.

3. Update Your Science

We now leave behind the domain of culture and spirituality and turn to the consciousness that inspires research and theory-formulation in science.

The concept of the world coming to light in the physical and biological sciences is not, as widely suspected, radically different, and perhaps even contradictory of the world-concept of the spiritual tradition. On the contrary, many of the tenets of quantum physics and quantum cosmology reaffirm age-old spiritual beliefs, such as, among others, the existence of space- and time-transcending connections among things and events, and the evolutionary drive toward coherence in us and around us. The Information Notes that follow tell you more.

Information Note (4): The Emerging Scientific World Picture

We can update the dominant world-picture of our time in light of what we are coming to know through science about the fundamental nature of the world. Here we outline the basic features of the world-concept emerging in science, reviewing in turn what cutting-edge science tells us about the physical world, the living world, and the world of mind and consciousness.

The Nature of the Physical World

Reviewing the insights science offers today regarding the nature of the physical world yields a surprising conclusion. The physical world is not what we thought it was. It is a quasi-miraculous world of universal interconnection and embracing coherence.

Classical physics gave us a mechanistic and atomistic view of the world. It reposed on Newton's universal laws of nature, as stated in his *Philosophiae Naturalis Principia Mathematica* in 1687. These laws became the foundation of the worldview of the modern age. They demonstrate with mathematical precision that material bodies are made up of mass points, and that they move according to mathematically expressible rules on earth, while planets rotate in accordance with Kepler's laws in the heavens. The motion of all masses is determined by the conditions under which motion is initiated, just as the motion of a pendulum is determined by its length and its initial displacement, and the motion of a projectile is determined by its launch angle and acceleration.

But classical physics is not the physics of our day. Although Newtonian laws apply to objects moving at modest speeds on the surface of the earth, the conceptual framework by which these motions and other observed phenomena are explained has radically changed. Today the smallest measurable and distinguishable units of the physical universe are not material entities, but quantized vibrations in a universal field. These are the quantum particles, or quantum waves — because they have both a corpuscular and a wave-aspect. The quanta themselves are made up of unobservable but theoretically distinguishable units called quarks. Quarks and quanta are intrinsically and instantly interconnected throughout space and time.

The idea of instant and intrinsic interconnection originated with the concept of entanglement advanced by Erwin Schrödinger in the 1930s. A seemingly metaphysical idea, its physical reality has been demonstrated over and over again in controlled experiments. Physicists have accepted the strange fact that quarks and quanta, and the structures built of them, are intrinsically entangled with one another. In its totality, the physical universe is an intrinsically and instantaneously interconnected whole — a view very different from the Newtonian universe of separate mass points.

The mechanistic–atomistic view of the universe was not the view held by Newton himself. Current research unearthed important studies where Sir Isaac Newton expounds a numerological, astrological, and inherently spiritual concept of reality. It appears that for Newton himself, researching the spiritual aspects of the world was more important than researching the physical aspects. This has been forgotten in the heat of the enthusiasm with which Newton's contemporaries greeted the scientific materialistic concept he developed, with its mathematically expounded laws and relationships.

Newton's followers inflated Newton's mathematical–mechanistic theory into an entire worldview. This paid off in the practical realm: the first industrial revolution has been squarely based on the root concepts and equations of Newtonian physics, testifying to their correctness. That they did not testify to their inflation into a general view of reality has not been immediately evident.

However, the inflated Newtonian worldview (which, as we now realize, was not Newton's own worldview but that of his followers) began to crumble at the end of the nineteenth century. The supposedly indivisible atom proved fissionable to a bewildering variety of components that, in the subsequent decades, dissolved in swirls of energy. Max Planck discovered that light, like all energy, is quantized and is not a seamless stream. Faraday and Maxwell came up with the theory of nonmaterial electromagnetic fields, and Einstein postulated that all events in space and time can be integrated in a four-dimensional continuum called spacetime.

The death knell of the Newtonian worldview was sounded in the 1920s with the advent of quantum physics. The quanta of light and energy that surfaced in ever more sophisticated experiments did not conform to our expectations of the behavior of macroscale objects. Their behavior proved to be more and more weird. Einstein, who received the Nobel physics prize for his work on the photoelectric effect (where streams of light quanta are generated on irradiated plates), did not suspect, and was never ready to accept, the weirdness of the quantum world. But physicists investigating the behavior of these packets of light and energy found that, until registered by a detecting instrument or another act of observation, quanta have no specific position, nor do they occupy a unique state. This seemingly weird proposition had to be accepted: the basic units of physical reality have no uniquely determinable location, and exist simultaneously in a superposition of several potential states.

Unlike the mass points of Newtonian physics — which are unambiguously definable in terms of force, position, and motion — the definition of the state of quanta had to be given by a wave function that encodes the superposition of all the states the quantum can potentially occupy. A quantum of light or energy (and subsequently, also of force) proved to be indeterminate as to the choice between its potential states. It manifests properties either as a wave or as a particle, but not as both. And its properties cannot be measured at the same time: if we measure position, for example, energy becomes blurred; and if we measure energy, position becomes indistinct.

However, as soon as it is observed, the quantum's indeterminate state is dissolved: it becomes determinate. It "actualizes" one of its potential states. In the language of physics, the quantum's superposed wave function collapses into the wave function of a classical particle.

What the weirdness of the quantum means in terms of our understanding of the nature of physical reality has been debated for nearly a century. The main points were made by pioneering physicists such as Niels Bohr, Werner Heisenberg, Louis de Broglie, and Erwin Schrödinger. Bohr advanced the principle of complementarity: a quantum has not one but two complementary aspects: wave and particle. Whether it appears as a wave or as a particle depends on the kind of questions we ask and the kind of observations we make. Heisenberg in turn put forward the "principle of uncertainty" according to which at any given time only one aspect of the quantum is measurable; a complete description is forbidden by nature.

The physical origins of complementarity and the interdiction of complete observation remained mysterious. According to Bohr, the very question whether the quantum is a wave or a particle "in itself" is not meaningful and should not even be asked. Quantum physicists must accept an intrinsic limitation: they can only deal with, in Nobel physicist Eugene Wigner's telling phrase, *observations*, and not with *observables*.

The Nature of the Living World

For most of the twentieth century, biology, the science of the living world, emulated physics in aspiring to be empirical and precise. In the classical Newtonian perspective, it ended up being materialistic and mechanistic. The holistic concepts that dominated the biology of the nineteenth century were condemned as speculative and "metaphysical." The mainstream biology of the twentieth century claimed that life emerges as the result of a random process without inherent aim. Chance-based alterations in the genetic structure of species are exposed to natural selection and generate the forms of life we encounter.

In the second half of the twentieth century, pioneering biologists attempted to transcend these notions. They began to consider the organism as a complex system with its own dynamics and guidance system. The organism is to be considered a whole system made up of interacting parts, such as cells, organs, and organ systems. These parts can be analyzed individually, and the analysis can show how their interaction produces the functions and manifestations of the living organism.

The above conception gave rise to molecular biology and modern genetics and encouraged the trend toward genetic engineering. The initial success of these methods and technologies was considered evidence for the soundness of the materialistic/mechanistic concept.

However, in the late twentieth century, further developments took place. Leading biologists noted that the alternative to materialism and mechanism is not a return to the nineteenth century notions of vitalism and teleology, but the development of an organismic approach to life. Their approach has been adopted by the leading process thinkers, among them Henri Bergson, Samuel Alexander, Lloyd Morgan, and Alfred North Whitehead, as an embracing philosophy of nature. Whitehead's concept of the organism — the "actual entity" — as a fundamental metaphor for entities in both the physical and the living world served as the rallying point for post-Darwinian schools in the new biology.

The organismic-holistic concept maintains that the organism has a level and form of integrity that cannot be fully understood by studying its parts and the interaction of its parts. The classical holistic concept, "the whole is more than the sum of its parts," is resuscitated. It became evident that when the parts of the organism are integrated within the whole organism, properties emerge and processes take place that are not the simple sum of the properties of the parts. The organism cannot be reduced to the interaction of its parts without losing these "emergent properties." They are the very features that make the biological organism a living entity.

"Coherence" is the concept that best expresses the new holism in biology. An organically coherent living system is not decomposable to its component parts and levels of organization. In the words of biophysicist Mae Wan Ho, such a system is dynamic and fluid, its myriad activities self-motivated, self-organizing, and spontaneous, engaging all levels simultaneously from the microscopic and molecular to the macroscopic. There are no controlling parts or levels, and no parts or levels to be controlled. The key concept is not control, but *communication*. Thanks to the constant communication of the parts in the organism, adjustments, responses, and changes needed for the maintenance of the whole can propagate in the organism in all directions at once.

Similarly to the entanglement of quanta in the physical world, in the living organism, instant correlations enable changes that propagate throughout the system, making even distant sites neighboring. This finding is incompatible with the mechanistic concept of the organism, where the parts are separate from one another and have definite boundaries and simple location in space and time.

Coherence in the living realm appears to be universal. It ranges from the smallest element in the organism to the full range of life on the planet. It encompasses multi-enzyme complexes inside cells, the organization of cells in tissues and organs, the polymorphism of living species within ecological communities, and the entire web of life in the biosphere. It ensures the coordination of the biosphere's myriad organic and ecological systems, and their coherent coevolution.

The concept of coherence in the living realm conflicts with the classical theory that the organism is the product of chance interactions among independent elements. The new concept is more than a philosophical or metaphysical tenet: there is evidence that pure chance (which would require the complete absence of causal links between the organism and its surroundings) is a theoretical construct; it is never the case in the real world.

The evidence on this score is wide-ranging. Random mutations in the gene pool cannot explain the evolution of life: complex structures have appeared on Earth in astonishingly brief periods of time. The oldest rocks date from about 4 billion years, and the earliest and already highly complex forms of life (blue-green algae and bacteria) are more than 3.5 billion years old. The classical theory cannot tell us how this level of complexity could have emerged within the relatively short period of about 500 million years. A chance mixing of the molecular soup in the primeval earth would have taken incomparably longer to produce the phenomena we observe. The assembly even of a primitive self-replicating prokaryote — a primitive, non-nucleated cell — involves building a double helix of DNA consisting of some one hundred thousand nucleotides, with each nucleotide containing an exact arrangement of thirty to fifty atoms, together with a bilayer skin and the proteins that enable the cell to take in and process food. This structure requires an entire series of coordinated reactions finely tuned with one another. Producing it is unlikely to be the result of chance interactions among separate elements.

Random mutations and natural selection may account for variations within a given species, but not for the evolution of complex living systems in the given finite time frame. Mathematical physicist Fred Hoyle pointed out that the probability that evolution would occur by chance is as likely as a hurricane blowing through a scrap yard assembling a working airplane.

Life comes about by massive and highly coordinated innovations in the genome, rather than by chance-based piecemeal variations in the genetic code. Genes do not work in isolation: the function of each gene is dependent on the context provided by all the others. The whole "ecology of genes" exhibits layers and layers of feedback regulation, originating both with the physiology of the organism and in the relationship of the organism to its environment. These "epigenetic" regulations can change the function of the genes, rearrange them, make them move around, and even mutate them. Major mutations are not due to a haphazard recombination of genes; they are responses of the epigenetic network of the organism to the chemical, climatic, and other changes generations of living organisms have experienced in their milieu. (The emerging insight combines a long-discredited thesis of Jean Baptiste Lamarck — *that the changes experienced by organisms can be inherited* — with a pillar of the theory of Darwin — *that inheritance is mediated by the genetic system*). It now appears that the experiences of the organism in its milieu affect subsequent generations of organisms. But this is not because the experiences would be directly communicated from one generation to the next, but because they leave their mark on the *epigenetic* system, the system that regulates the functioning of the genetic system. Through the epigenetic system, the imprint of lived experiences is handed down from one generation to the next.

The discovery of epigenetic links between the genome and the organism, and between the organism and the world around it, suggests that the living world is not the harsh domain of classical Darwinism, where every species competes for advantage with every other. Rather, life evolves through what biologist Brian Goodwin called "the sacred dance" of the organism with its milieu. Subtle strains of this dance extend to all the species and ecologies in the biosphere.

We are not Newtonian machines. We are not separate from each other and from our environment; we are part of an interconnected system with an intrinsic evolutionary drive and space- and time-transcending interconnections. We are elements in a quasi-living self-evolving universe, where every element interacts with every other, and jointly creates systems of ever-increasing complexity and coherence.

The Nature of Consciousness

Can we put the question regarding the nature of consciousness on a par with the question concerning the nature of the physical world and even of the living world? Philosophers and sages have often claimed that mind is something that is radically different from matter and life, and it is in a category of its own. But today, we realize that the human mind, more exactly the phenomenon of consciousness by which we experience it, is part of the natural world. It is just as real as energy, frequency, and information, and far more real than matter.

The human mind, that is, our consciousness, is primary. We do not experience the world directly, except through intuition or enlightenment. Information about the world comes to us through the flow of sensations that accompanies us throughout our lives — the flow we experience as *our consciousness.*

Consciousness is the most familiar, but also the most mysterious element of our life. It is mysterious because it is not clear what it is, or what its origins are. Is the flow of sensations that makes up our consciousness generated by our brain? Or does it extend in some way beyond the brain and the body?

Until a few years ago, nobody other than esoteric people would have subscribed to the proposition that consciousness is more than a product of the brain. But today, there is a new insight dawning among physical and life scientists and consciousness researchers: consciousness is nonlocal. It exists in association with the brain, but it is not produced by and confined to the brain.

The Classical Concept of Consciousness

In modern society, the accepted view is that consciousness is produced by the brain. In the context of classical physics, there is no place for consciousness in the world. All that exists in the universe is bits of matter in space and time. Consciousness is an epiphenomenon: it is generated by a real phenomenon, but it is not real in itself. In this respect, consciousness is like the electricity generated by a stream of electrons in a turbine. The electrons are real, the turbine is real, but the electricity generated by them is a secondary phenomenon. It disappears, after all, when the electrons cease to stream in the turbine. The existence of electricity is contingent on the working of the turbine, and the existence of consciousness is contingent on the working of the brain. Consciousness no more exists in a dead brain than electric charge exists in a stationary turbine.

We do not see, hear, or taste electricity; we know it only by the effect it produces. This is said to be the same with consciousness. We experience the flow of sensations, feelings, and intuitions we call consciousness, but we do not perceive consciousness itself. No amount of scrutiny of the brain will disclose anything we could call consciousness. We only find gray matter with networks of neurons firing in sequence. In creating the sequence of the flow of electrons, the brain generates the sensations we experience: feelings, and volitions. When the brain's operations are damaged or reduced, consciousness is distorted, and when the brain stops working, consciousness ceases.

For the classical concept, there is nothing miraculous, or even mysterious, about the presence of consciousness in the universe. Human consciousness is the product of the workings of the human brain.

The New Concept of Consciousness

The above concept of consciousness is generally held in the contemporary world, but it is no longer supported by science. The classical concept of consciousness is ready for the dust-heap.

The turbine concept of consciousness is a hypothesis, and as all hypotheses, it can be maintained if it is confirmed by observation. The predictions generated on the basis of a hypothesis must be confirmed by observation. In this instance, the critical prediction is that consciousness ceases to exist when the brain stops working.

On first sight, this prediction is confirmed by observation: when cerebral functions come to a halt, consciousness disappears. This is not directly observed, but it is a reasonable inference from what we do observe. People who are brain-dead do not seem to possess a working consciousness.

This does not admit of exception. We can no more account for the presence of consciousness in a dead brain than we could account for the presence of electric charge in a stationary turbine. Evidence to the contrary would place in question the basic tenet of the classical concept of consciousness. But evidence to the contrary does exist. It surfaced in clinically controlled, rigorously protocolled experiments. There is real and credible evidence that in some cases consciousness does not cease when brain functions do.

The most widely known form of the evidence is furnished by people who have reached the portals of death but returned to the ranks of the living. In some cases, their consciousness appears to persist even when their brain functions are "flat." Many temporarily brain-dead people report having had conscious experiences during their near-death episode. NDEs — near-death experiences — are surprisingly widespread: in some cases, they are reported by up to 25 percent of the people who experienced a condition near death.

Are NDEs cases of veridical recall, or are they fantasy? Repeated experiments suggest that they are veridical. NDE reports have been confronted with experiences the subjects would have had if their brain would have been functioning normally, and in a significant number of cases, the recalled experiences and the "would have" experiences exhibit a remarkable and more than random match.

There are indications that conscious experience persists not only during the temporary cessation of brain function, but also in its permanent absence: when the individual is fully and irreversibly dead. These surprising experiences became known as ADEs: after-death experiences. The evidence for them is offered by mediums in deeply altered states of consciousness. In these trance-states, they appear able to communicate with deceased persons. They "hear" the deceased people recount their experiences after they died.

Reports of ADEs have been subjected to systematic scrutiny, exploring the possibility that the mediums would have invented the messages, or picked them up from living persons through some form of extrasensory perception. In a non-negligible number of cases, the theory that they were invented by the mediums could be ruled out: the messages contained information the mediums were unlikely to have invented themselves. And accessing such information through ESP (extra-sensory perception) is a logical assumption, but ESP itself is in need of corroboration by reliable evidence.

Given the amassed evidence, we are logically obliged to accept that some near-death and after-death experiences are veridical. This calls for a radical revision of the mainstream concept of consciousness.

The new concept is that consciousness is more than a product or by-product of brain function. "Our" consciousness is a local and temporary manifestation of a consciousness that is a real element in the real world. More and more consciousness researchers join pioneering brain scientists, psychologists, and psychiatrists who make this bold assertion.

That consciousness exists beyond the brain has been maintained by a number of world-renowned scientists. Erwin Schrödinger, for example, did not hesitate to say that consciousness does not exist in the plural: the overall number of minds in the world is one. In his last years, Carl Jung came to a similar conclusion. The psyche is not a product of the brain and is not located within the skull; it is part of the one-universe: of the *unus mundus*. In David Bohm's quantum cosmology, the roots of consciousness are traced to the deeper reality of the cosmos: the implicate order. A number of contemporary scientists, such as Henry Stapp, maintain and elaborate this concept. Consciousness is nonlocal: it is a cosmic phenomenon. The cosmos is one, and if consciousness is a cosmic manifestation, then consciousness is one.

In the emerging concept, the flow of sensations we call consciousness is as real as energy, frequency, amplitude, phase, and information in the universe, and more real than matter. The brain is not a material turbine that generates consciousness, and consciousness is not its product or by-product. Consciousness is cosmic; the brain is only its receiver — more exactly, its transcriber. The most reasonable conclusion is that "my" consciousness is a local manifestation of the universal consciousness that pervades the universe.

Information Note (5): Current Findings of Research on Consciousness, Cosmos, and Evolution—*with contributions by Kurt Johnson, Robert Atkinson, and Jude Currivan*

Consciousness Research

Findings in current research on consciousness show that the evolution of consciousness takes us from one consciousness state to another, through a transformative process of moving from a consciousness based on separation toward a consciousness based on wholeness.

There is a pattern underlying this process; it defines and assists the orderly movement of evolving consciousness. With transformation at its core, this pattern is central to many ways of knowing and is understood as a means of merging opposites into a new unbroken, unified whole. Mythology, mysticism, ritual and psychology share a three-part process leading to the transformation and restoration of wholeness.

These transformations express variations on the same pattern. Wholeness on the social level is only possible as a transformative process connecting all the personal and collective parts of the system into a new, balanced, and harmonious whole within which all parts consciously share the common purpose of contributing to the ongoing betterment of the world—what Kabbalists call Tikkun Olam, the work of repairing the world or restoring the world to wholeness.[8]

New Cosmology Research

The cutting edge of the universal science of cosmology supports the view offered in this book. The known Universe emerges from deeper, nonphysical realms of cosmic intelligence. Key to these insights are the holographic non-locality principles reflected in the recent Nobel Prizes in Physics to Roger Penrose (2020) and to John Clauser, Alain Aspect and Anton Zeilinger (2022). The cosmos is a system of meaningful "*in-formation*" that literally *in-forms* and manifests holographic and non-locality principles such as the appearance of the entire energy-matter domain and multidimensional spacetime. As a result, the latest information emerging in science regarding all scales of existence and in multiple fields of research is converging with the wisdom teachings of the Upanishads of ancient India as well as with the pioneers of quantum physics, to reveal our Universe as a great and finite "thought" in the infinite and eternal mind we name the Cosmos. Here mind and consciousness are not something we *have* but what we and the whole world really *are*. They transform our understanding, describing a living and sentient Universe as a non-locally unified entity, existing meaningfully and evolving purposefully.

Our Universe began to evolve some 13.8 billion years ago, not in the presumed chaos of a Big Bang, but more likely as the first act of a fresh pulsation — a Big Breath. As space expanded and time flowed, it has embodied an evolutionary impulse *to* evolve, from simplicity to complexity and ever-greater levels of diversity, individuated self-awareness and perceived collective interdependence.

In the story of our planetary home, Gaia, as the ancient Greeks named their goddess of the Earth, the evolutionary impulse of our Universe continued its emergence for the last 4 billion years. Gaia has emerged through innately collaborative relationships, intermeshed cycles and multi-level co-evolutionary partnerships throughout the planetary *gaiasphere* comprising the rocks and minerals of the geosphere, the waters and ice of the hydrosphere, the varying composition of the atmosphere and the abundance, diversity and increasing complexity of the whole biosphere.

As embodied in the evolutionary progress of our Universe, Gaia, rather than being driven by random occurrences, is all-pervasively and innately relational and intelligently and coherently guided by in-formational signals, flows and processes. Here and now, this majestic 13.8-billion-year universal journey embodied in humanity, reached a further potential in the pivotal upshift to conscious evolution.[9]

New Research on Evolution

A large part of the present (mis)understanding of the nature of evolution reaches back a century and three-quarters in regard to the theories of Charles Darwin. In 1859, his ground-breaking *The Origin of Species* brought biological evolution into popular discourse and opened the door to the awareness that all things evolve, even on the level of society and culture. However, "Social Darwinists" (primarily politicians, economists and business magnates) turned his theory of evolution in a particular direction, focusing (often perniciously) on the survival of the fittest and the competition needed to sustain our presence in the biosphere. Becoming a pervasive worldview, this turn legitimized such developments as segregation, racism, genocide, and war and violence.

Darwin himself had much to say about both social and biological evolution. Having been a divinity student, he came to embrace the principle that all life comes from the same source and is part of the "great Tree of Life." Historically, and in the context of twenty-first century evolutionary science, Darwin is to be remembered above all for his view that cooperation, not competition, leads to creation of larger and larger circles of unity.

In 1871, in *The Descent of Man*, Darwin clearly stated that his view of social evolution is built on cooperation on all levels:

> As man advances in civilization, and small tribes are united into larger communities, the simplest reason would tell each individual that he ought to extend his social instincts and sympathies to all members of the same nation, though personally unknown to him. This point being reached, there is only an artificial barrier to prevent his sympathies extending to the men of all nations and races.

Clearly, Darwin viewed social evolution as directed toward a long-desired outcome, extending the natural law of cooperation and the golden rule from the individual to the global level. As Robert Atkinson wrote in *A New Story of Wholeness* (pp. 8, 9), Darwin's grand vision of social evolution calls for a leap of individual consciousness to conduce to a leap in collective consciousness. In 2022, Kurt Johnson together with other authors honored David Loye, a Darwin scholar who had written extensively on the misunderstandings and misrepresentations of Darwin's theories.[10]

In what is now called the "post-resolution" explication of a newer and fuller understanding of the process of evolution, the series "The Foundational Questions in Science" by Yale/Templeton in 2015, tackled and resolved the issue of Darwinian natural selection *against* the acceptance of Social Darwinism. By "post-resolution," its authors — including such eminent scholars as Harvard's E. O. Wilson and State University of New York's David Sloan Wilson — meant just that. They declared that "everything else is commentary." This statement is so famous that if one internet searches for "Evolution everything else is commentary," the references come right up. Wilson and Wilson, representing the high tide of the new understanding in evolutionary science, had previously re-written the "theoretics" of Sociobiology (the biology of social organisms) in 2007 based on the new views.

It is now understood there are three kinds of natural selection operating in nature: "Darwinian" (or Individual), "Group," and "Multilevel." Only the first makes selfish selections; the latter two make selections "for the good of the whole." This is how altruism evolves. Science now understands that the *definition* of "fitness" changes as a system complexifies — from competition as fitness to cooperation as fitness. In cultural evolution, it is cooperation as fitness. Of course, all three kinds of natural selection sustain survival. This puts modern evolutionary science in step with the New Physics, understanding that the operative rules of a process change as the system complexifies.

Displaced by this new paradigm has been another long-reigning view of conventional science — the (anthropomorphic) idea of "the selfish gene." This, too, is relegated to a lesser place within the larger system as explicated in current books such as those of Harvard's E. O. Wilson (*The Meaning of Human Existence*, 2015) and J. Arvid Agren of the Lerner Research Institute of the Cleveland Clinic (in his recent *The Gene's Eye View of Evolution*, 2021). The emerging views, including "inclusive fitness theory," accounts for the presence of a variety of evolved forms of altruisms, from bees to humans.

In sum, "the selfish gene" metaphor does not work well for understanding cultural evolution, using only one criterion of "life," which is replication. The classical view of "fitness" regards only biological reproduction, whereas in cultural evolution, "replication" is largely a question of selecting the right ideas from humankind's symbolic repertory. Life is more than replication; it is also a "creative advance into novelty," to use a phrase of philosopher Alfred North Whitehead.

Unfortunately, the assumptions of Social Darwinism persist, even if they do not dominate today, especially in business and politics. D. S. Wilson, in a book subtitled *Completing the Darwinian Revolution*, begins with a chapter entitled "Dispelling the Myth of Social Darwinism." Writing on how entrenched this misunderstanding has become, he asks if it can ever be turned around in politics, business, and economics.[11] This turn-around is indeed unlikely in the absence of the wave of fundamental change we see as the coming upshift.

PART THREE

PEACE ON THE PLANET—THE VISION

CHAPTER 7

AN ACHIEVABLE VISION: DATELINE 2050

It is time to complete this guide to promoting our conscious evolution on the planet with a vision that lends a wider and deeper perspective to this enterprise. The vision proposed here may appear utopian on first sight, but will prove relevant as we focus on the diverse tasks of an upshift to conscious evolution.

Here is an "achievable vision" — the image of a peaceful and sustainable world emerging by the middle of the twenty-first century in the conscious embrace of the web of life on the planet.

The Vision of the Social Order

The decisive feature of the world of 2050 is that it consciously seeks harmony with life on the planet. In this regard, it is essential that the new world is clearly oriented to evolution in nature and the universe. It is neither an undifferentiated totality, nor a sequence of separate elements. It is a world that is globally whole and locally diverse.

Sovereign nation-states, the inheritance of the Modern Age, have given way to a transnational world where nations are only one, even if an important, level of the social order, without laying claim to sovereignty.

The human world is networked, but not monolithic. It is structured as a Chinese box of administrative and decision-making forums, where each forum is embedded in each higher forum but has its own sphere of authority and responsibility. The political world is not a hierarchy, for the decision-making forums at the various levels have their own autonomy and are not subordinated to higher levels.

In some areas — including trade and finance, information and communication, peace and security, and environmental protection — decision-making is entrusted to global forums. This, however, allows a significant level of autonomy on local, national, and regional levels. Taken in its totality, the political world is a "heterarchy": a multilevel sequentially integrated structure of distributed decision-making aimed at global cooperation combined with regional, national, and local spheres of authority and leadership.

The diverse yet cooperative world is a sequence of self-reliant communities with multiple links of communication and cooperation. Individuals join together to shape and develop their local community. These communities participate in a wider network of cooperation that includes, but does not cease at, the level of national states. Nation-states are themselves part of regional social and economic communities, coming together in the United Regions Organization, the global-level body created through the reform of the United Nations Organization. Its members are not nation-states but the continental and subcontinental economic and social unions that integrate the interests and programs of nation-states. These include the European

Union, the North American Union, the Latin American Union, the North-African Middle-Eastern Union, the Sub-Saharan African Union, the Central Asian Union, the South and Southeast Asian Union, and the Australian-Asia-Pacific Union.

The principle of subsidiarity holds sway throughout the multilevel system: decisions are made on the lowest level at which they are effective.

The *global level* is the lowest level in regard to ensuring peace and security and regulating the global flow of goods, money, and knowledge. It is also the level for coordinating the information that flows on global networks of communication. Its objective is to harmonize policies dedicated to ensuring the integrity of the processes that maintain equilibrium in the biosphere.

The *regional level* is indicated for the forum for policies that coordinate the social and political aspirations of nations. Regional economic and social organizations provide the forum for the representatives of member nations to coordinate their interests and aspirations in view of resolving the problems of their people.

The *national level* is appropriate for the local tasks and functions traditionally entrusted to national governments. National organizations operate without claiming unconditional sovereignty for themselves; they are embedded in the regional and global-level forums and take due account of the decision made by them.

On the *local level*, forums bring together the elected representatives of urban as well as rural communities. They coordinate the workings of the social and political institutions of towns, villages, and rural regions within the framework of the administrative and decision-making system composed of forums on the national, the regional, and the global levels.

The Individual and the New Order

Lifestyles

Some people are well off, but nobody is superrich. Simpler lifestyles are the rule and not the exception; they are the fruit of an upshifted culture that guides people's aspiration for living a healthy life with consideration for others and without ostentation.

The diversity of lifestyles finds expression in the sphere of interpersonal communication, in contact with nature. The basic aspiration is personal growth and development in the embrace of concentric spheres of life and decision-making starting with the family and extending sequentially to local community, region, and nation, to the global community of all nations and regions.

People live longer and healthier but do not trigger an explosion of the population. They realize that it is irresponsible to create families larger than the replacement level. In most parts of the world, a two-child family is the popular dimension of fertility.

The human population is moving toward equilibrium between fertility and mortality at a low and for the present sustainable level. This offers benefits to everyone. With modestly sized families, parents are better able to care for their children and ensure that they grow into healthy persons with sufficient education and access to information to live well.

Lifeways are becoming ecologically conscious. As people are reoriented from self-centered satisfactions brought by individual consumption toward personal growth and interpersonal development, energy and material requirements in the world are diminishing to more sustainable levels. And, as people work together to improve their shared living and working environment, community life enjoys a renaissance. People, both women and men and young and old, rediscover a deeper dimension in their consciousness, the dimension of the evolutionary impetus. They search for coherence and oneness, and ultimately love, as the grounding values of their existence.

Morality

Lifeways remain socially, culturally, and geographically diverse. Religious beliefs, cultural heritage, technological development, levels of industrialization, climate, and nature are all factors that enter into and enrich the panoply of lifeways. Yet, beyond the diversity there is a shared morality. Personal and interpersonal growth and development are to respect the limits of an acceptable quality of life for all people in the human community.

The shared morality goes beyond the pragmatic liberalism proclaimed by the Anglo-Saxon philosophers, among them Jeremy Bentham, John Locke, and David Hume. In their view, people can pursue their interests as long as they respect the rules that safeguard life in a civilized society. "Live and let live" is the motto. People can live in any way they please, as long they do not break the law.

In the year 2050, people realize that in an interdependent and delicately balanced world, the classical forms of liberalism are misplaced. Letting everyone live as they please as long as they keep within the law entails a serious risk. The rich and the powerful may consume an ever more disproportionate share of the resources to which the poor also have claim, and may harm the environment that is a common resource for all.

Rather than "live and let live," a code of behavior is coming to light that is better adapted to conditions on the planet than classical liberalism. It replaces liberalism's "live and let live" with Gandhi's "live more simply so others could simply live."

Gandhi's injunction is further specified. The principal concern is not with the intrinsic simplicity of the way people live, but with the impact of the way they live on others, and on nature. This impact must not exceed the capacity of the planet to provide for the needs of all people. Simple lifestyles are to be favored not just because of an intrinsic preference for simplicity, but because simple lifestyles are more likely to remain within the limits of adequate human resource availability in the biosphere. The new moral code takes into account the impact of the human species on Earth — a planet of great wealth but of finite resources. The emerging moral code is summed up in the injunction: *live within the limits of the resource-use that permits others to live as well.* As the new moral code takes hold in the mainstream of society, cutthroat competition for selfish and self-centered ends is replaced by a spirited rivalry in the context of shared goals and common interests.

Expecting that people abide by the new moral code does not call for people to become selfless angels. Living in a way that permits others also to live does not mean that everybody could live in the same way with the same material standard of living. There are differences in wealth and standards of living, but these differences are moderated by the moral injunction regarding the limits of how we can live our lives.

The new morality respects the right of all people to live a life of dignity, spared the deprivations that plagued the poor in the recent past. Being moral does not call for being self-denying — it allows everyone to strive for excellence, beauty, and personal growth. But in the context of an interdependent and finite planet, the enjoyments and achievements of life are to be defined in relation to the quality of enjoyment and level of satisfaction they provide, and not in terms of their monetary cost and the quantity of materials and energy they consume.

Beliefs

The traumas and crises that hallmarked the world of the early twenty-first century have not been forgotten: people know that what they believe shapes the world. A periodic reexamination of our core beliefs is a precondition of safeguarding the better world we seek to, and could, create.

The beliefs and convictions that emerge in the reexaminations are very different from the beliefs that hallmark today's world. The decisive elements of the beliefs that shape the 2050 world can be summed up in a few bullet points.

- We are part of the web of life on Earth, and the web of life is part of us. We are what we are in our communication and communion with the beings that emerge and evolve in the web of life of this planet.

- We are more than skin-and-bone material organisms. Our bodies with their cells and organs are manifestations of what is truly us: self-sustaining, self-evolving, dynamic beings arising and evolving in interaction with all other self-evolving dynamic beings around us.

- We are one of the highest, most evolved manifestations of the drive toward coherence in the universe. Our core essence is this universal drive. Recognizing it and aligning with it is both our duty and our privilege as conscious beings.

- There are no absolute boundaries and divisions in the world, only phase transitions where one set of relations yields prevalence to another. In our bodies, the relations that integrate our cells and organs into a dynamic and coherent whole are prevalent. Beyond our bodies, the relations that drive toward coherence and wholeness with the communities of living beings gain prevalence.

- The separate identity we attach to people is a convenient convention that facilitates interaction with them. The whole gamut of concepts and ideas that separates our identities from the identities of other persons is but an arbitrary convention. There are only gradients distinguishing individuals from each other and from their environment, and no categorical divisions and boundaries.

- In the final count, there are no "others" in the world: we are all living beings, and we are all part of each other. Our family and community are just as much who we are as the cells and organs of our bodies.

- Collaboration, not competition, is the royal road to sustain us and all the beings who inhabit the Earth. Collaboration calls for empathy and solidarity, and ultimately for love. Collaboration inspired by love is the way to achieve health and wellbeing for ourselves, and for all the beings with whom we share The Planet.

- Attempting to advantage the beings we know as "us" through ruthless competition with the beings we know as "others" is a grave mistake: it damages the integrity of the embracing whole that frames our lives. When we harm "others," we harm ourselves.

- The idea of advantaging ourselves, even our families, communities, and nations, without regard for the beings we used to regard as "strangers" or "foreigners," needs to be rethought. Patriotism, if it aims to eliminate adversaries by force, and heroism, even in the well-meaning execution of patriotic aims, is an unwise and dangerous aspiration. A patriot and a hero who brandishes a sword or a gun is an enemy to everyone, himself or herself included. Comprehension, conciliation, and forgiveness are the hallmarks of courage, not championing the ambitions of some without concern for others.

- "The good" for anybody in the human community is not the possession of riches. Wealth in any material form is but a means for curating our existence in the embrace of the community of life. As exclusively "mine," wealth commandeers part of the resources all living beings need to share. Exclusive wealth is a threat to the communities of life, including the communities of those who hold it.

- The true measure of our accomplishment is the measure of our sharing, not of our having. Sharing enhances existence in the communities of life, whereas possessing creates division, invites competition, and fuels envy. The share-society is the norm for the communities of life; the have-society was typical only of the modern age, and it was an aberration.

- We and our fathers and forefathers have been guilty of an aberration in the evolutionary path of humanity, and as conscious and responsible members of humanity, we recognize that correcting this aberration is our moral duty and historic responsibility. Beyond the pursuit of deeper love and higher meaning, building a society aligned with life on the planet is the most vital task of our life.

The Global Charter of the Year 2050[12]

Preamble

- We, the people of the planet, are at a crossroads in our evolutionary journey. We can choose to make great music and come into harmony as one, or continue on the current path of discordant chaos with the inevitable results — it all depends on whether we are willing to attune with humanity and the natural world.

- In this singular moment in history, we must choose between the values of an old paradigm structured in competition, individualism, and materialism, or embrace a new mindset rooted in cooperation, the good of the whole, and a higher level of consciousness. We must look toward our indigenous roots of harmony and oneness with Gaia, with each other, and with Spirit, however we define it, for a balance of the feminine and the masculine and with an eye toward the wellbeing of future generations. Now is the time to choose a new way forward, one of peace and cooperation with the world around us, both inside and out.

- To do any less, to ignore the current conditions of our time — the rampant fear, anger, exploitation, violence, social and financial inequality, and the rapid deterioration of our environment — is to continue on a path toward disaster, and to include ourselves potentially in the rapidly unfolding sixth extinction. If we see that our current universe is an aberration of the original vibration and it produces the cacophony of our times, it will be clear to us that our mindset is dangerously out of tune. Instead of cooperation within the band, leaders motivated by profit and power play their own instruments to their own tunes at the expense of the collective harmony that creates collective wellbeing.

Article 1

- Our current governance framework reflects a musical score written from the perspective of a mechanistic and hostile universe, with a "winner-takes-all" system of values. Our world of nation-states competing for the perceived limited resources has obliterated our natural order of oneness with each other and the planet, and held us captive to a political machine dependent on strong borders, armaments, and violence. The illusion of separation has infiltrated our souls and allowed us to think that the music of life itself is a competition for volume at any cost, as if the musician who plays or sings the loudest is the most deserving at the expense of those who offer a more subtle or nuanced contribution. Now is the time for a collective song of reason and harmony to be sung within a new system of politics.

Article 2

- In the emergent sacred governance in the global orchestra, fear dissolves into our natural state of love. This love is the simple resurgence of the golden rule that has existed from time immemorial in indigenous and holistic societies — in essence, to live in harmony with all fellow musicians. Our current belief that individual rights are sacrosanct is a mistake. What is good for the individual may not be good for the whole, whereas what is good for the whole orchestra is always good for every individual player. This is the moment when each individual must retune her instrument, so its sound will be in harmony with all the players in the planetary orchestra.

- We ask that the leading figures of the self-governance of humankind become humble and committed conductors in service to the whole. Consider some specialized professions: doctors, teachers, engineers. There are high standards that must be met to call oneself a medical practitioner. It requires a commitment of years of study, examination, apprenticeship, and ongoing education. The Hippocratic oath, one of the oldest binding documents in history, continues to be held sacred by physicians. Let us envision a new day when the formerly ego-driven governors of nation-states are guided by a similar universal principle. Envisage the day when a sacred code of ethics is adopted, a code that enables leaders to be caretakers of a melodious, peace-loving, nature- and universe-loving society.

- The new ethics calls to our evolving consciousness to embrace the journey toward a higher state of being. Our inherent altruistic nature will manifest in a safer and more compassionate world in which we will begin to play in tune with our deepest instincts, creating a world of cooperation with a win-win condition for all.

Article 3

- Our evolution as a species embraces healing and reconciliation. To overcome the fear and greed that has driven political thought in the past, we strive to align ourselves with a frequency of vibration that brings us back into balance with the human spirit and with Mother Earth. We strive to expound our cultural and artistic impulses to honor the highest qualities of our endeavors within a political process anchored in sacred service to the good of the whole. The new stories of success are achieved by those who do the most good for society and the planet.

- The emergent and restructured global governance system is based on a fortified United Nations with a World Federalist Charter, adhering to the Earth Charter and a new Constitution for the New Paradigm in Governance. Funded by a scaled system based on per capita income, the new world governance will provide relief for the poor and underserved. No longer will credit and privilege be given to those soloists who prefer the sound of their own voices at the expense of the harmony of the whole. At long last, the human symphony will resound with the frequency of our original sacred vibration.

Article 4

- Behold the new mindset: a celebration and embodiment of goodwill and cooperation, based on the ideals of truth, beauty, and goodness. Sworn to sacred duty, our leaders will be trained and guided by a council of globally elected governors, highly skilled practitioners of right statesmanship. Unity is found in a new code of inclusion extending to all races, ethnicities, cultures, sexual identities, indigenous beliefs, and states of being. There is a place and a purpose for everyone in the new composition of universal citizenship.

- Leaders who embody the new mindset understand the power of language and honor the responsibility of engaging in truthful communication on behalf of humanity and the planet. Instead of using human resources to manage divisiveness, new energy is generated from the cohesiveness of the governance process, allowing social justice and equal opportunity to contribute to an elevation of consciousness on an accelerated scale. Just as some countries have transformed by shifting the perspective from "me" to "we," all nations with the new mindset now surge forward with measurements of happiness. The new leaders pave the way for universal health care and education, allowing everyone to live a vital and balanced life. This new mindset is holistic — honoring the good of the whole as its first priority.

Article 5

- Future generations will be born into a world honoring their unique form of being so we all could reach our highest expression: a world in peace, upheld by the World Federalist Constitution and maintained by the supervision of the United Nations, with an equitable distribution of power representing all peoples of the planet.

- With leaders assuring the basic necessities for everyone, the rising tide of collective consciousness can be upheld by a guaranteed supply of safe and environmentally friendly food, clean drinking water, and fresh air for the entire human population, living in sustainable balance with nature. In this potentially noblest of professions, the politicians of the new mindset establish a sacred contract that each member of the human community can sign as a global citizen, activating a society based on direct democratic principles that guarantee equal voice and participation for all people. The contract is to include all parts and elements of society. It is to empower women to take their rightful place as equal partners leading the way to a better future drawing on the divine feminine. As such, love and unity is the message of the new anthems, issuing a call for political bodies to take action and heal the wounds inflicted in history.

Article 6

- We hereby declare that each one of us has the responsibility and now also the opportunity to sing together and energize humanity to an ever-evolving higher state of consciousness. Alongside our politicians, we are all active participants in crafting this new vision of universal citizenship, engaged in transforming our current system that operates on a love for power into a new system impelled by the power of love.

- Embodying our birthright to fulfill our sense of purpose for the good of the whole becomes a rite of passage. Within the new paradigm of politics, our innate goodness and respect for collective wellbeing empower all people and bring all people in the world to a deeper understanding of the universe as a living system in balance with human communities and their natural environment. The evolution of consciousness that comes as a result of political coherence economizes energy on all scales and brings our world into collective harmony. The enlightened politician is the conductor of the symphony created by all the people of the human family.

By the middle of the 21st century, the pursuits of power and wealth and their related gratifications as the be-all and end-all of human existence have been transcended. An essential level of harmony and peace have returned at last to planet Earth.

POSTSCRIPT

THE UPSHIFT HAS STARTED!

There is significant evidence today that the upshift of the human community toward the conscious guidance of its evolution has moved from the plane of hope and aspiration to that of action.

In order to document this hopeful assessment, this writer, and his friends and associates, in particular The Club of Budapest, The Laszlo Institute of New Paradigm Research, World Upshift Organisation, the Evolutionary Leaders Circle of the Source of Synergy Foundation and the Editors of Light on Light Press, reviewed the domain of humanistically-oriented global activism and came up with a roster of organizations they believe merit to be named "Upshifting Organizations." They make up the first "Catalog of Upshifting Organizations."[13]

This Catalog, with its entries from all over the world, offers meaningful indication that the domain of globally oriented social activism has begun to provide practical instruments and solid arguments for guiding the evolution of the global community toward peace and harmony and a higher level of wellbeing.

CATALOG OF UPSHIFTING ORGANIZATIONS

The Love Peace Harmony Foundation (Canada)
Founded by Master Zhi Gang Sha, the Foundation is a non-profit enterprise devoted to service to humanity by creating a more loving, peaceful, and harmonious world. Its mission is to empower people, organizations, and communities to cultivate an environment of love, peace, and harmony. It is committed to taking the concept of world peace from theory to practice, dedicating each day to inner peace so as to create a ripple impact among families, friends, communities, organizations, countries, and ultimately the entire human family.

Bertalanffy Center for the Study of Systems Science (Austria)
The BCSSS is dedicated to advance systems concepts and systemic approaches to achieve innovative solutions for a sustainable development. We work in trans-disciplinary processes at the interface of science – humanities – engineering and design to create a better and more sustainable future for all, addressing the global challenges we face today.

Global Education Futures (Netherlands)
The GEF Initiative is an international collaborative platform that brings together shapers and sherpas of global education to discuss and implement the necessary transformations of educational ecosystems for thrivable futures.

EARTHwise Center (Mauritius)
EARTHwise Centre serves to steward and actualize the possibilities for thrivable worlds and futures, by developing the necessary capacities, systems, governance, tools, and pathways for a planetary civilization.

World Upshift Organisation (UK)
The coordinating body for the World Upshift Movement, a global initiative working with individuals and partner organisations around the world to increase awareness of the challenges facing humanity and the need to embrace new ways of living to address these challenges.

The Club of Budapest (Hungary)
Founded in 1993, the Club of Budapest is an international association dedicated to developing a new way of thinking and a new ethics that will help resolve the social, political, economic, and ecological challenges of the 21st century. The Club initiates a dialogue between different belief systems and worldviews in order to co-create and develop effective strategies for responsible and sustainable action with a global focus. The Mission of the Club of Budapest is to be a catalyst for the transformation to a sustainable world through promoting the emergence of planetary consciousness and interconnecting generations and cultures.

The Laszlo Institute of New Paradigm Research (Italy)
The Laszlo Institute researches, develops and communicates the essential aspects of the new way of thinking and acting we need at this critical time: the new paradigm. The mission of the Institute is to foster open transdisciplinary inquiry into current science-based conceptions of the human being and his and her world. The Institute brings together open-minded and dedicated scientists and lay people from all parts of the world and all walks of life, to develop the emerging ideas and communicate them to people in their particular fields as well as to society at large.

Humanity's Team (USA)

Humanity's Team is a global non-profit organization focused on helping people throughout the world awaken to the interconnectedness — or Oneness — of everything in the Universe, so they can embody that awareness in every aspect of their lives.

AITIA Institute (Singapore)

We believe in reimagining the 21st century world view of leadership and business to become more effective in bringing about a positive impact to the communities around us. Our organisation is built on creativity, mindfulness and consciousness — and purposed to empower you to make a meaningful difference to your community.

HeartMath Institute (USA)

For more than 25 years, HeartMath Institute has been researching the heart-brain connection and learning how the heart influences our perceptions, emotions, intuition and health. HeartMath helps you tap into the power and intelligence of your heart — your heart's intuition — which awakens you to the best version of yourself.

GreenHeart (USA)

Since 1985, Greenheart International has been a catalyst for global transformation through the facilitation of cultural exchange programs, eco-fair trade purchasing, personal development opportunities, volunteer service initiatives, and environmental advocacy projects. Our mission of connecting people and planet to create global leaders drives all that we do in each of our branches: Greenheart Travel, Greenheart Shop, and Greenheart Exchange.

May Peace Prevail On Earth (USA, Japan)

The May Peace Prevail On Earth movement is a grassroots global movement to inspire, and re-awaken the inherent consciousness of love, peace and harmony which exists in every one of us. It is a movement to bring inner peace of mind and to foster peace in the world at large, allows us to sincerely focus on our mutual desire to serve, create and manifest true peace on earth while transcending our differences and celebrating our common humanity.

Simpol Solution (UK)

Simpol (Simultaneous Policy) is an international governance movement — led by you, the citizens of the world — that sees global cooperation as the answer to the threats to our very existence. With Simpol, we have a new, powerful way to make governments act — a way they cannot ignore. Simpol is a global citizens' movement built around a simple concept; when citizens drive nations to act together at the same time, we can achieve the global collaboration needed to solve the challenges we face.

Synchronistory (Germany)

From the Me Generation to the We Generation, Planet E needs a ReGeneration! With its captivating Cirque du Soleil influence, dazzling interstellar backdrop, a confluence of interactivity, immersive media, and otherworldly elements, Synchronistory© offers an unprecedented global event-phenomenon of epic scope and depth; a Party for the Planet honouring Every Living Being in a music-inspired edutainment spectacular broadcast live worldwide.

The Four Winds Society (Chile, Peru, USA)

Founded by Dr. Alberto Villoldo, The Four Winds Society offers the world's most thorough training in Shamanic Energy Medicine combined with cutting-edge practices in nutrition, biology and neuroscience. Over the past 25 years, we have trained and mentored more than 10,000 students from all walks of life — scientists, construction workers, nurses, doctors, psychologists, massage therapists, and others — to dream a new world into being.

Four River Institute (Ecuador)

Cuatro Rios (Four Rivers) Institute is dedicated to curating contemplative and experiential learning for the advancement of consciousness, ecology, human transformation, and leadership. The Institute will be forged through partnerships with ancient and indigenous wisdom traditions, new thought leaders, spiritual scientists, and transformational educators and innovators.

The Hague Center (Netherlands)

The Hague Center consults, coaches and partners with individuals and organizations who want to learn, grow and co-create together. THC fosters networks and people who desire to take up leadership in their projects. THC brings them together as the foundation of a Meshwork with a shared intention and the willingness to serve a larger purpose.

Goi Peace Foundation (Japan)

The Declaration for All Life on Earth is the guiding vision of the Goi Peace Foundation. It describes our common responsibility as members of a global community and sets forth universal principles to realize a sustainable and peaceful world in the 21st century. Our aim is to share the vision of the declaration and to encourage all people to apply its values and principles in their individual lives and in their specialized fields of activity.

Academy for the Study of Future Civilizations (Republic of Korea)

The Global Academy for Future Civilizations holds regular conferences to "establish common values and new plans for humanity and the global community." By providing an arena for pan-global exchange and research on modern societal phenomena in politics, economics, society, culture, and science, the Academy is expediting the formation of discourse on alternative civilization. For the past 30 years, its Peace Conference has contributed to the global expansion of peace research, education, and campaigns.

The Arison Group (USA)

For over three decades, The Arison Group, founded by Shari Arison, has promoted Doing Good on every activity level: business, philanthropy, spirituality, books, art, and unique international ventures and projects.

Good Deeds Day (USA)

Good Deeds Day is a global movement of people who are dedicated to doing good. Since 2007, millions of people and thousands of organizations from over 108 countries unite annually to volunteer and Do Good. Every year, it supports global changemakers who desire living in a better world to take impactful action by providing tools, inspiration, and global network.

The Foundation for Conscious Living (USA)

The Foundation for Conscious Living, founded by Gay Hendricks, is a non-profit organization devoted to empowering people to embody Authenticity, Response-ability, and Appreciation: in partnership, community, politics, society, and the planet. We're creating a world in which everyone enjoys a flow of appreciation and co-creation, in an evolutionary (instead of fear-based) context.

Dancing Star Foundation (USA)

Dancing Star Foundation ("DSF") mission, founded by Michael Charles Tobias, is focused on international biodiversity conservation, global environmental education, and animal protection. The Foundation is involved in active ecological restoration efforts and intensive environmental field research — much of which is disseminated in a multitude of lectures and symposia, and all manner of publications.

Art of Living Foundation (India)

Sri Sri Ravi Shankar's Art of Living Foundation based in India promulgates Gurudev Sri Sri Ravi Shankar's vision of personal and social transformation through mental health and wellness has ignited a global movement in over 150 countries, uplifting the lives of more than 450 million people.

Blue Ribbons Worldwide (USA)

The "Who I Am Makes A Difference"® Blue Ribbon Ceremony was born out of Helice "Grandma Sparky" Bridges' desire to create a world where all people would feel connected, valued, and loved. They are part of a global team helping to Unite Humanity Through the Power of Love for this generation and all generations to come!

Tariq Khamisa Foundation (USA)

The Tariq Khamisa Foundation (TKF) was founded in honor of victims of youth violence. Uniting families who have experienced this tragedy, it is dedicated to teaching and inspiring forgiveness, hope and peace in youth and setting them on a path towards opportunity. Worldwide it has connected over 500,000 youth, empowering them to make positive choices for their lives and futures.

UNIFY (USA)
UNIFY unites Global Meditation Movement by promoting local meditation, yoga and spiritual communities to come together for a meditation flash mob in a prominent public location. Working through local chapters, millions of people participate globally on days dedicated to our common humanity to create a Unified Field of peace and service.

Earth Day/ Earth Gratitude (USA)
Growing out of the first Earth Day in 1970, Earth Day is the world's largest recruiter to the environmental movement, working with more than 150,000 partners in over 192 countries to drive positive action for our planet. Its Earth Gratitude Project celebrates each Earth Day with games, artwork, eZines, Virtual Festivals and much more.

Mark Gober Productions (USA)
Mark Gober is the author of *An End to Upside Down Thinking* (2018), which won the IPPY award for best science book of the year. He is also the author of *An End to Upside Down Living* (2020), *An End to Upside Down Liberty* (2021), *An End to Upside Down Contact* (2022), and *An End to the Upside Down Reset* (2023); and he is the host of the popular podcast *Where Is My Mind?* (2019).

New Dimensions Foundation (USA)
The New Dimensions Foundation is an educational organization supported by listeners to such popular broadcasts as Mark Gober and others. The foundation provides support for the New Dimensions Radio program series, which is internationally-known and highly acclaimed for its transformational content.

Marianne Williamson and Project Angel Food (USA)

Marianne Williamson founded Project Angel Food which has delivered more than 14 million meals to sick or dying homebound patients since 1989. The group was created to help people suffering from the ravages of HIV/AIDS. Marianne has also worked throughout her career on poverty, anti-hunger and racial reconciliation issues. In 2004, she co-founded The Peace Alliance supporting the creation of a U.S. Department of Peace.

Always Mystic (USA)

Greg Leveille's company, Always Mystic, was formed to help humankind as it moves towards a new Golden Age of Spirituality. Despite the problems and the challenges in the world, there is always a tender, compassionate, middle-way through and beyond the chaos. There is always a mystic approach that anyone can follow. Always Mystic is creating and publishing a library of essays, books, newsletters, podcasts and videos which will help spiritually minded seekers, practitioners and teachers to easily understand the introductory and the highest levels of spiritual wisdom.

The Consciousness and Healing Initiative (USA)

The Consciousness and Healing Initiative (CHI) is a non-profit collaborative of scientists, healing and health practitioners, educators, and artists, who work together to place healing in the center of healthcare, and self-care. CHI offers exclusive online webinars, workshops and courses with leaders in health and healing.

My Green Pod (UK)

My Green Pod is for anyone who wants to live a more sustainable lifestyle but doesn't know where to start. Browse or buy ethical alternatives to everyday products and discover simple sustainable switches that work. Read up on the latest environmental issues and events in our news section, or flick through digital issues of our magazine.

Eternea (USA)

The vision of Eternea is to be one strategy in a larger broader effort to profoundly transform human nature thence human civilization. Such a transformation would result in replacing avarice with altruism, duality with oneness and divisiveness with unity. Eternea proposes to accomplish its vision by serving as an impetus to elevate human awareness, values, attitudes and behavior through facilitation of a critical mass awakening in which false illusory perceptions of the larger all-encompassing reality are replaced with true, accurate perceptions of its actual nature.

The World Academy of Art & Science (USA/International)

The WAAS was founded in 1960 by a group of eminent scentists, spiritual leaders, and other intellectuals. The Academy serves as a forum for reflective scientists, artists, and scholars dedicated to addressing the pressing challenges confronting humanity today independent of political boundaries or limits, whether spiritual or physical — a forum where these problems can be discussed objectively, scientifically, globally, and free from vested interests or regional attachments to arrive at solutions that affirm universal human rights and serve the common good of all humanity. WAAS is founded on faith in the power of original and creative ideas — Real Ideas with effective power to change the world.

Global Consciousness Project (USA)

The GCP is an international, multidisciplinary collaboration of scientists and engineers. We collect data continuously from a global network of physical random number generators located in up to 70 host sites around the world at any given time. The data are transmitted to a central archive which now contains more than 15 years of random data in parallel sequences of synchronized 200-bit trials generated every second. The purpose is to examine subtle correlations that may reflect the presence and activity of consciousness in the world. We hypothesize that there will be structure in what should be random data, associated with major global events that engage people's minds and hearts.

California Institute of Integral Studies (USA)
CIIS is an accredited university that strives to embody spirit, intellect, and wisdom in service to individuals, communities, and the earth. CIIS expands the boundaries of traditional degree programs with transdisciplinary, cross-cultural, and applied studies utilizing face-to-face, hybrid, and online pedagogical approaches. Offering a personal learning environment and supportive community, CIIS provides an excellent multifaceted education for people committed to transforming themselves, others, and the world.

Chopra Foundation (USA)
The Chopra Foundation seeks to advance the cause of mind/body spiritual healing, education, and research through fundraising for selected projects. We offer teaching and resources for health and spirituality for disadvantaged individuals and communities, specifically through our concrete commitments to: at-risk children, low-income women and teenagers, prisoners, educating healers, and initiating scientific research. The Chopra Foundation's Mission is to participate with individuals and organizations in creating a critical mass for a peaceful, just, sustainable, and healthy world through scientifically and experientially exploring non-dual consciousness as the ground of existence and applying this understanding in the enhancement of health, business, leadership and conflict resolution.

The Galileo Commission

The Galileo Commission's remit is to open public discourse and to find ways to expand science so that it can accommodate and explore important human experiences and questions that science, in its present form, is unable to integrate. Following widespread consultation with 90 advisers representing 30 universities worldwide, we have published the Galileo Commission Report, written by Prof. Dr. Harald Walach and entitled *Beyond a Materialist Worldview — Towards an Expanded Science.* The report has been widely endorsed as a groundbreaking document, and we encourage you to read it for yourself and spread the word among your professional networks.

Villaggio Globale (Italy)

The Global Village is a non-profit scientific and cultural social promotion association of which the main purpose is education for self-awareness and psychophysical wellbeing and personal growth for a more ethical, human and sustainable world. It offers awareness groups and training courses which are open to all people who want to undertake a path of human knowledge, internal search and transformation.

Emoto Peace Project (Japan)

The purpose of the Emoto Peace Project (EPP) is to educate people, especially children, of the true nature and importance of water through the Picture Book "The Message from Water" by Dr. Masaru Emoto, and his other works and research. Our mission is to share in an informative, entertaining, awakening way, how water structure changes to reflect the vibrations of whatever we are thinking and feeling.

Jane Goodall Institute (UK)

JGI is a global community conservation organization that advances the vision and work of Jane Goodall. It is based on the credo that by protecting chimpanzees and inspiring people to conserve the natural world we all share, we improve the lives of people, animals and the environment. JGI makes a difference through community-centered conservation and the innovative use of science and technology. It works closely with local communities around the world, inspiring hope through the collective power of individual action.

Agape International Spiritual Center (USA)

Since its doors opened in 1986, Agape's active teaching and practice of the New Thought-Ageless Wisdom tradition of spirituality has expanded into a trans-denominational movement and community comprised of thousands of local members and global live streamers. Through Rev. Michael Beckwith's weekly services, Agape's University of Transformational Studies and Leadership classes, ministries and other outreach programs, the heart of Agape reaches deep into local and global communities teaching individuals about the transforming, healing power of prayer, meditation, and selfless service.

Manchester Bidwell Corporation (USA)

MBC is an empowering atmosphere of art, light and music. Our guiding principles and diverse programming transform the lives of our community, adults-in-transition and Pittsburgh-area youth. These principles are at the heart of our Founder & Executive Chairman Bill Strickland's educational model and, in his own words, are the cure to the cycle of poverty. We implement these principles in many ways — adult career training, youth arts education and social enterprise — but the end result is a better way forward for our community.

Ethical Markets (USA)

Ethical Markets' mission is to foster the evolution of capitalism beyond current models based on materialism, maximizing self-interest and profit, competition and fear of scarcity. Ethical Markets© showcases the organizations, trade associations, shareholder activities, the mutual funds and pension funds asset managers, financial planners, venture capital groups, innovative technologies and companies, as well as this vision of maturing, socially-responsible, ethical capitalism fitting humanity's aspirations for a more peaceful, just and ecologically sustainable world.

The Institute of Noetic Sciences (USA)

The mission of the Institute of Noetic Sciences (IONS) is to reveal the interconnected nature of reality through scientific exploration and personal discovery. Serving this purpose, IONS provides a research center and direct-experience laboratory specializing in the intersection of science and human experience and an array of public educational programs and media.

Scientific and Medical Network (UK)

The SMN is a creative international forum for lifelong transformative learning and change. The Network is part of a worldwide contemporary movement for spiritual emergence, bringing together scientists, doctors, psychologists, engineers, philosophers, complementary practitioners and other professionals in a spirit of open and critical enquiry to explore frontier issues at the interfaces between science, consciousness, wellbeing and spirituality.

The Shift Network (USA)

Our Vision is to empower a global network of evolutionary change agents through media, education, and resources featuring leading wisdom keepers and visionaries. We empower people on a journey of personal growth over time and provide a platform for an emerging culture to connect, collaborate, and co-create. We aim to accelerate the shift to a world where each and every one of us has the opportunity to liberate our full creative potential.

The Sounds True Foundation (USA)

The objective of the Sounds True Foundation is to create equitable access to wisdom-based books, tools, and practices.

Academy of Inner Science (USA)

Founded in 2008 by Thomas Hübl, the Academy of Inner Science aims to connect the wisdom of the inner world with the knowledge of the outer world. The Academy offers training modules, workshops, study groups, and facilitation training. These programs support individuals seeking a framework for their own personal development as well as the opportunity to cultivate a deeper transpersonal awareness and participate in collective evolutionary development.

WholeWorld-View (UK)

Merging science and spirituality, we aim to bring the most up to date science and experiencing of our great interconnectedness. This information, we hope, grounds, inspires and empowers you on your journey to express and embody your unique and individual diversity, feel your belonging and powerfully know and spread awareness of our fundamental unity.

Source of Synergy Foundation (USA)

The Source of Synergy Foundation is a not-for-profit educational organization whose purpose is to synergize individuals, organizations and efforts by tapping into the infinite source of collective consciousness, creativity and potential for the common good. Our intention is to support the release of synergistic energy that will exponentially expand and create a global ripple effect in planetary consciousness. We all recognize that when individuals, organizations, communities and nations unite in a shared sense of responsibility for the common good their collective efforts have a far greater effect on the whole.

R3.0 (Germany)
We are a global common good, not-for-profit platform that promotes Redesign for Resilience and Regeneration and crowdsources open recommendations for necessary transformations across diverse fields and sectors, in response to the ecological and social collapses humanity is experiencing.

Wellbeing Economy Alliance (UK)
We are a solidarity network of global change organizations including a number of signatory countries designing an economic system based upon holistic wellbeing.

Seat of the Soul Institute (USA)
We believe that a great transformation in human consciousness has begun, our evolution now requires spiritual growth, and spiritual growth requires conscious choices. We provide programs and tools that help you create emotional awareness, responsible choice, intuition, trust, and spiritual partnerships — partnerships between equals for the purpose of spiritual growth (creating authentic power). Created by Gary Zukav and Linda Francis in 1999.

SINE (USA)

SINE (Synergized Impact Network Exchange) creates synergy and acts as a global collaborative community that fuels collective empowerment and unprecedented unified action.

Compassion Games (USA)

Compassion Games is a community engagement experience that invites people around the world to inspire one another to reveal and promote acts of compassion that better our lives, our communities and all life on Earth.

Cosmolocalism (EU)

Cosmolocalism is a pilot research project to test cosmo-localism "Design Global, Make Local," a decentralized production business model based on sharing of knowledge.

Principled Societies Project (USA)

The Principled Societies Project an evidence-based model for an alternative local economy based upon a dual currency system of standard fiat currency plus a local token exchange system.

The Eco Group (South Africa)

The Eco Group is a regenerative property development company that has developed a new turnkey, sustainable model for community development in the South, including every aspect of community from financing, to job creation in the local economy, to all necessary services and infrastructure.

International Institute of Applied Systems Analysis (Austria)

The IIASA is leading systems analysis scientific institution, pioneering simulation and Integrated Assessment Models.

The World in 2050 (TWI2050) (Austria, Sweden)

A partnership between IIASA, Stockholm Resilience Centre and the Sustainable Development Solutions Network focused on finding leverage points to attain the UN SDGs within a short timeframe using a new, high-level Integrated Assessment Model combining climate, economic and ecological models.

Tellus Institute (USA)

The Tellus Institute was established in 1976 as an interdisciplinary, not-for-profit research and policy organization that brings scientific rigor and systemic vision to critical environmental and social issues. Tellus has conducted 3,500 projects throughout the world, becoming an internationally recognized leader in the emerging field of sustainable development. Tellus is now focused on advancing a just and sustainable planetary civilization. This Great Transition would entail a fundamental shift in human values and in the ways we produce, consume and live. The key is balancing the rights of all people now alive with those of future generations and the wider community of life.

Great Transition Stories (USA)

Great Transition Stories is a virtual hub for illuminating the larger, often invisible, archetypal stories of our world, which can help us make sense of these times. By bringing to light the deeper patterns we are in and where they lead, we begin to have more choice in how we can consciously evolve our collective story towards wholeness, wellbeing, justice, beauty, and regenerative culture.

Action for Happiness (UK)

Founded in 2010 in London, Action for Happiness had the simple but radical idea that we can uplift the quality of life in our societies if we each make happiness our primary goal.

Loving Classrooms (UK)

Based in London and working internationally, Loving Classrooms delivers positive relationship education which identifies and boosts the innate goodness in all students, so that they interact with love and kindness, and crave the wellbeing and fulfillment of all individuals and humanity.

Universal TheoGnostic Society (USA)

This international non-profit civil society dedicated to shamanic mysticism has dedicated 30 years to studying ancient aspects of humanity, spirituality and mysticism that include techniques used by the mystics and sages of all ages. Shaman Omar is Director of Speakers and travels the world leading shamanic breath, meditation and shamanic medicine retreats.

The Elikia Hope Foundation (Democratic Republic of Congo)

The Elikia Hope Foundation is an organic humanitarian effort, launched approximately four years ago by Queen Diambi Kabatusuila Tshiyoyo Muata of the Democratic Republic of Congo. Compelled by her strong sense of purpose, The Queen has committed to mobilize local non-profit organizations familiar with the challenges of the small villages and communities with very modest means. Their mission is to identify issues such as shortages of clean water, health care, and education, then transform ideas to solutions with financial and material support from conscientious benefactors.

Action for Happiness (UK)

Action for Happiness is a movement of people taking action to create a happier and kinder world. It brings people together and provides practical resources and evidence-based skills for happier living, the sense of belonging, and commitment to personal action to create more happiness for all peoples around the world.

Loving Classroom (UK)

Loving Classroom delivers Positive Relationship Education (PRE) which identifies and boosts the innate goodness in all students, so that they interact with respect and kindness, and crave the wellbeing and fulfilment of all individuals and humanity. It was founded by David and Naomi Geffen.

Academy for Future Science (USA)

The Academy for Future Science is a non-profit corporation that examines new scientific ideas for the future. The principal goal of the Academy is to provide all people with educational and scientific tools that will help them meet the resulting challenges.

AgeNation, LLC (USA)

AgeNation is a global organization committed to providing the very best in information, inspiration and engagement to a rapidly growing audience of older GenXers, Boomers and elders who are committed to living vital, successful and conscious lives.

All Things Connected (USA)

Dr. Julie Krull serves as a midwife for the evolution of consciousness, whole systems health, and a whole worldview. She works with evolutionary change-agents — co-creating greater connection and wholeness — as a best-selling,

Nautilus Award-winning author, speaker, consciousness coach, mentor, host of "The Dr. Julie Show: All Things Connected" and founder of Good of the Whole.

Bridges In Organizations (USA)

Bridges in Organizations brings diverse work combined with anthropology expertise to organizations, addressing everything from culturally-sensitive customer service to navigating messy conversations — conflict that can arise when operating from inaccurate assumptions or unconscious bias.

The Center for Partnership Systems (USA)

The Center for Partnership Systems (CPS) — formerly the Center for Partnership Studies — is dedicated to research, education, and building tools to construct economic and social systems that support human beings and the planet that sustains us. This site provides a wide array of resources about the history and foundations of Partnership Systems that will empower you to apply partnership principles in your own family, community, workplace, and government.

Children of the Earth (USA)

Children of the Earth inspires and unites young people, through personal and social transformation, to create a peaceful and sustainable world. One Earth…with all her Children smiling!

Choosing Earth (USA)

Choosing Earth offers many resources to help you learn more about the challenges and opportunities of our time of great transition. The Choosing Earth Project recognizes the world confronts much more than a climate crisis; we face a whole systems crisis that includes the mass extinction of species, growing shortages of fresh water, extreme inequities of wealth and wellbeing, and much more.

Community of the Mystic Heart (USA)
We seek to help each other grow and deepen in spiritual life and to be a prophetic voice for the emergence of a more just, sustainable and peaceful world. We nurture the continuing refinement and advancement of the Interspiritual message brought forth by Brother Wayne Teasdale and his teachers, and we encourage each other in living out our vows to actualize the Mystic Heart, in service to the One, in which is included all of creation.

Contemplative Life (USA)
Contemplative Life is a central hub that brings many different practices under one umbrella, to easily find what's right for you and connect with others of like mind.

Create Global Healing (USA)
Founder Lori Leyden, PhD, MBA, is an internationally known trauma healing expert and spiritual guide. Dr. Leyden works with successful leaders and influencers committed to becoming heart-centered leaders in service to global healing. She also works in traumatized communities that have experienced genocide, war, and school shootings.

Everyday Knowings (USA)
Founder Rev. Dr. Heather Shea is a Spiritual Leadership Coach for women executives, entrepreneurs, and evolutionary leaders. She connects people to their inner wisdom and uncovers blocks that prevent them from stepping into their highest, authentic self for greater impact in their lives and the world.

Garden of Light (Mexico)

Garden of Light is a global community deeply rooted in a shared spirituality that transcends differences of circumstance, nationality, tradition, culture and even religion. The Garden of Light offers a virtual home for this community so that it can become visible for the powerful force that it truly is in uplifting the human spirit and approaching the global challenges we face as one global family.

Global Coherence Pulse (USA)

Global Coherence Pulse is a science-backed social collaboration to *Pulse the Planet* with the frequencies of love and compassion, joy and appreciation, being monitored by global instrumentation networks to help science tell the story of our interconnectedness and of the power of our Collective Heart.

Good of the Whole (USA)

Good of the Whole is a growing community with a global mission and shared purpose. Good of the Whole creates whole-systems alternatives for the world's biggest problems, so that every person has an opportunity to evolve to their highest potential.

Hygeia Foundation (For Health, Science and the Environment) (Scotland)

Hygeia Foundation supports holistic health education and research, fosters a common respect for all life on earth and promotes awareness of the interconnectedness of all creation. The Hygeia Foundation supports and sponsors a variety of projects that are aligned with this mission, particularly those that promote the principles and practice of sustainability.

Integral City Meshworks (Canada)

Integral City Meshworks is a global constellation of communities of practice that nurtures cities as human hives. Through placecaring and placemaking, Integral City Meshworks inspires a Planet of Integral Cities as living, integral, evolutionary human systems, to become Gaia's Reflective Organs. An Integral City paradigm views the city as a whole living system. It is the Human Hive. Like the beehive is for the species of the honey bee, the Integral City is the collective habitat for the human species.

Interstellar Community Foundation (USA)

The Interstellar Community Foundation is an organization made up of a worldwide network of conscious individuals working together to manifest the Vision of the Interstellar Universities and Universe Cities, co-creating the communities of the future whose purpose is to provide humanity with the necessary tools, skills and consciousness to grow into our cosmic nature, preparing humanity to interact with civilizations beyond our planet. The Vision has a 3-fold purpose: Liberating our full Human Potential, Achieving Planetary Consciousness, and Taking our Place in the Cosmic Community.

Islands of Coherence Community Network (USA)

Islands of Coherence Community Network is a heart-centered membership network, made up of communities of practice sharing evolutionary tools for embodied coherence, social synergy and planetary regeneration. Islands of Coherence Community Network aims to be an ecosystem of epic individuals, projects and solutions for the great shift of our species.

Karmic Warrior (USA)

The mission of Karmic Warrior is to teach time-proven principles and practices of Yoga wisdom that free us from continual cycles of ups and downs in life (karma) and give us direct access to lasting inner peace, clarity, and connection so that we can awaken to our true nature and contribute to the flourishing of humanity.

Light on Light Publications and Media (USA)
Light on Light, a non-profit from the Interspiritual Dialogue Network, publishes books and e-magazines, and hosts VoiceAmerica ("The Convergence") broadcast media. Its books are an imprint of Sacred Stories; its free e-magazines from ISSUU are *Light on Light*, *Convergence*, and *Conscious Business.*

Living Cities Earth (USA)
Living Cities Earth is an interdisciplinary action research network, connecting 10,000 cities and a web of integral experts serving Gaia's wellbeing.

NewStories (USA)
The purpose of NewStories is to help people, organizations, communities and systems navigate the tides of change towards wellbeing, compassion and deep collaboration. We do this through looking at the current stories in place and gently guiding shifts towards a new way of being.

One Humanity Institute (Poland)
One Humanity Institute — a City of Hope… from I to We to ONE… from Hate to Hope… The overarching goal for this vision is to lay the groundwork for global solidarity that gives rise to what it means to be One Humanity. The Institute offers structured learning opportunities in a variety of forms for all ages, and will focus on the UN 17 Sustainable Development Goals, inter-and intra-faith studies, inter-cultural understanding and cooperation, conflict resolution, trans-rational problem solving, reconciliation, entrepreneurial

social impact projects, and leadership skills for the rising potential of the empowered individual.

One Planet Peace Forum (USA)
One Planet Peace Forum offers a universal platform for an annual interdisciplinary, interspiritual gathering for living into a culture of peace. Understanding peace holistically as both an inner and outer evolutionary process and the culmination of an age-old promise, its mission is to inspire cooperative action toward building the future envisioned by the world's spiritual and wisdom traditions.

Peace Pentagon (USA)
The Peace Pentagon is a retreat and training center located in the Blue Ridge Mountains of Virginia along the ancient New River. We are committed to pluralistic and progressive values and host educational programs that provide hope for humanity. The Peace Pentagon also serves as a hub for planning and organizing regional, national, and global peacebuilding and social justice campaigns. Our mission is to help YOU gain the information and tools to be a better advocate for the issues that matter to YOU!

Prosocial World (USA)
While Prosocial World is based on science, it is not just for scientists. It is also for activists, idealists, pragmatists, visionaries, and contemplative change agents; in short, anyone who has a prosocial worldview. As such, it uniquely places the vision of spiritual seekers, who embark on different paths to self-discovery to consciously evolve a more harmonious and regenerative world, on a foundation of the most recent developments in evolutionary science.

Purpose Earth (Spain)

Purpose Earth's mission is to fund and mentor purpose-driven people and projects with creative solutions to our global challenges.

Rainbow Circle (USA)

Rainbow Circle is a community supporting a system that contextualizes and synergizes people, knowledge, organizations, and missions within a 12-domain multi-colored circle. Each archetypal domain contains keywords in a digital space, so anything can be mapped into a domain depending on its corresponding keyword. Through this design, Rainbow Circle illustrates how many visions can coherently align as one to regenerate the Earth and evolve humanity.

Self Care to Earth Care (USA)

The purpose of Self Care to Earth Care is to provide space for the leading voices and activists across the interspiritual, eco-spiritual, sustainability and other transformative landscapes; to vision and effectuate future programs, events and initiatives across these areas of passion; and to provide space for various constituencies and sectors to gather together that are committed to self-care and earth care and are shaping a new, ecological society and culture.

Spiritual Life TV Channel (USA)

The Spiritual Life TV Channel features wisdom teachings from many spiritual traditions and gives a practical focus that shows how a person can use these teachings to live a more spiritual life.

The Great Turning at Findhorn (Scotland)

The Great Turning Initiative at Findhorn is an online spiritual education and resource center to support individuals and organizations to navigate and actualize The Great Turning — humanity's epochal transition from a life-destroying society to a life-affirming global family.

The Heart of the Healer Shamanic Mystery School (Peru)
The Heart of the Healer Shamanic Mystery School is committed to the co-creation of a heartfelt sacred community informed by the shamanic star-seeded wisdom of our cosmic origins. We support the eco-spiritual evolution of humankind through soul-honoring initiatory apprenticeships in the Pachakuti Mesa Tradition, Goddess Consciousness, and Ancestral Star Knowledge.

The Interspiritual Dialogue Network (USA)
ISD is the original interspiritual organization of Brother Wayne Teasdale, the renowned interspiritual pioneer. It continues events and initiatives for interfaith and interspirituality, its well known newsletter, and is the parent of Light on Light Publications and Media. Its website centers on the message of *The Coming Interspiritual Age.*

The Interspiritual Multiplex (USA)
The Interspiritual Multiplex is a far-flung and dynamic network formed as of 2005 from the various constituencies and groups inspired by the work and writing of Brother Wayne Teasdale. It aims at carrying forward to a wider audience worldwide his vision of interspiritual dialogue and interspirituality as outlined in *The Mystic Heart: Discovering a Universal Spirituality in the World's Religions.*

The Interspiritual Network (USA)
The Interspiritual Network formed from combined constituencies of interfaith and interspiritual pioneers like Thomas Merton, Thomas Keating,

Wayne Teasdale and many others. It includes resources from, and about, nearly one hundred spiritual leaders, teachers, authors and activists. It has been home for the "Dawn of Interspirituality," "Interspiritual Mandala" and other initiatives.

The Oracle Institute (USA)

The Oracle Institute is an educational charity dedicated to building a new world based on Social Justice, Interfaith Unity, and a Culture of Peace. Our mission is to advance this global transformation by hosting pluralistic programs and anchoring progressive values.

The RIM Institute (USA)

RIM® (Regenerating Images in Memory) is a body-centered, transformational technique that frees you of negative thoughts, feelings and memories, so you are empowered to live your best life. Deborah Sandella PhD, RN is the originator of the ground-breaking Regenerating Images in Memory (RIM®) Method, which is a heavily-backed neuroscience tool proven to reduce stress and improve quality of life.

Sacred Stories (USA)

Sacred Stories is an award-winning conscious book publisher and multimedia company that believes wisdom coupled with the power of story — written, spoken, and lived — allows us to deepen into the Mystery of our souls. Their visionary publishing imprints include Light on Light Press, Haniel Press, and flagship Sacred Stories Publishing.

Touching the Stillness Ministries (USA)

Touching the Stillness Ministries is a global spiritual organization, synonymous with mindfulness and meditation practices designed to create exhilarating and meaningful connections, with that which we call God, as well as deepen our awareness in ways that will transform our lives.

Ubiquity University (The Netherlands)

Ubiquity mission is grounded in the reality that history has reached a critical moment and people everywhere need to be nurtured with new mindsets, skillsets and tool sets to work together to solve global challenges. Ubiquity has an innovative combination of intellectual and artistic learning in which all students are required to engage in equal measure to balance the left and right hemispheres of the brain and thereby engage in integrated learning.

UNITY EARTH (Australia)

UNITY EARTH is a growing network of groups and organizations coming together to empower solutions for unity, purpose and peace worldwide. Our calling is to weave threads of unity within the colorful diversity of the human family and the ecosystems that sustain us.

Wise Planet Media (USA)

Wise Planet Media helps to create a wiser and more just world through award-winning media storytelling.

Soul of Money Institute (USA)

The work of Soul of Money Institute is inspired by the powerful life experiences of Lynne Twist as a global fundraiser for The Hunger Project and the Pachamama Alliance and as detailed in her book, *The Soul of Money*. The Soul of Money Institute addresses the dysfunction and suffering that most people have in their relationship with money, and we are bringing a new level of consciousness to the way money impacts our life and society. The Soul of Money Institute was founded to create a context of sufficiency, responsibility and integrity for individuals and organizations in their relationship with money.

In view of the emergence and rapid growth of the above and similar organizations, this book concludes with the optimistic but well-supported affirmation: *The upshift of humanity has started!*

NOTES AND REFERENCES

1. References: H. Küng, [as recorded in] *Christianity: Essence, History, Future* (Continuum, 1995 edition); "The Nine Points of Agreement Among the World's Religions" in N. Miles-Yepez [Ed.], *The Common Heart: An Experience of Interreligious Dialogue* (Lantern 2006); "The Nine Elements of a Universal Spirituality" in W. Teasdale, *The Mystic Heart: Discovering a Universal Spirituality in the World's Religions* (New World Library, 1999) as updated also in K. Johnson and D. R. Ord, *The Coming Interspiritual Age* (Namaste Publishing, 2013); P. Hawkin, *Blessed Unrest: How the Largest Movement in the World Came into Being and Why No One Saw It Coming* (Viking, 2007).

2. References: McKay, A. et al. (2022). Exceeding 1.5°C global warming could trigger multiple climate tipping points. Science, 377 (6611), DOI: 10.1126/science.abn7950; Rockström, J., Steffen, W., Noone, K. et al. (2009). A safe operating space for humanity. Nature 461, 472–475 (2009). https://doi.org/10.1038/461472a; Wang-Erlandsson, L., Tobian, A., van der Ent, R.J. et al. (2022). A planetary boundary for green water. Nat Rev Earth Environ 3, 380–392. https://doi.org/10.1038/s43017-

022-00287-8; IPCC. (2022). Climate Change 2022: Impacts, Adaptation and Vulnerability. IPCC Sixth Assessment Report by Working Group 2. IPCC. Accessed 22 July 2022 via https://www.ipcc.ch/report/ar6/wg2 /.

3. References: PEW, Harris, Yankelovich and *Financial Times* cited in Chapter 3 in K. Johnson and D. R. Ord, *The Coming Interspiritual Age* (Namaste Publishing, 2013). Wikipedia statistics at "Democracy Index"/ Wikipedia.

4. Sir Oliphant's message was transmitted in a letter to Michael Ellis of Australia. This writer is grateful to Dr. Ellis for sharing it and agreeing to its publication.

5. These Calls are excerpted from the *Manifesto on the Spirit of Planetary Consciousness* drafted by the present writer in collaboration with the Dalai Lama in the year 1996.

6. References: S. J. Freeland and L. D. Hurst, "The Genetic Code Is One in a Million," (*Journal of Molecular Evolution* 47, no. 3 (January 1998): 238–48); D. Noble, "Evolution Beyond neo-Darwinism: A New Conceptual Framework," *Journal of Experimental Biology* 218 (April 2015): 7–13; G. Battail, "Error-correcting Codes and Information in Biology," (*Biosystems* 184 (October 2019): 103987; J. A. Shapiro, *Evolution: A View from the 21st Century* (FT Press, 2011).

7. References: D. S. Wilson and K. Johnson, "Integrating an Evolutionary Vision of the Future with "Hard" Science"; E. Laszlo, "Reasoning and Experiencing Our Way to Oneness"; and articles by G. Braden, D. Chopra, B. Lipton in R. Atkinson, K. Johnson and D. Moldow [Eds.], *Our Moment of Choice: Evolutionary Visions and Hope for the Future* (Beyond Words, Simon & Schuster, 2021); re: R. Penrose, "Facts 2020," Nobel Prize.org.

8. References: R. Atkinson, from the Preface of *The Holomovement: Embracing Our Collective Purpose to Unite Humanity* (Light on Light Press, 2023); R. Atkinson, *A New Story of Wholeness: An Experiential Guide for Uniting the Human Family* (Light on Light Press, 2022) pp.xiii-xxi; E. Laszlo, "Reasoning and Experiencing our Way to Oneness" in R. Atkinson, K. Johnson and D. Moldow [Eds.], *Our Moment of Choice: Evolutionary Visions and Hope for the Future* (Beyond Words, Simon & Schuster, 2021); S. Grof, "A Brief History of Transpersonal Psychology" (Wayback Machine Internet Archive); K. Wilber, *The Eye of the Spirit: An Integral Vision for a World Gone Slightly Mad* (Shambhala, 1998); K. Wilber, *The Religion of Tomorrow: A Vision for the Future of the Great Traditions-More Inclusive, More Comprehensive, More Complete* (Shambhala, 2017); A. L. Combs and K. Wilber, "Wilber-Combs (W-C) Lattice" in K. Wilber, *Integral Spirituality* (Integral Books, 2007); A. L. Combs, "Remembering David Loye" (*Interdisciplinary Journal of Partnership Studies* 9(2), 2022).

9. References: J. Currivan. *The Cosmic Hologram: In-formation at the Center of Creation* (Inner Traditions, 2017; audiobook, 2022); J. Currivan. *The Story of Gaia: The Big Breath and the Evolutionary Journey of our Conscious Planet* (Inner Traditions, 2022); re: R. Penrose, "Facts 2020," Nobel Prize.org; re: J Clauser, A. Aspect and A. Zeilinger, "The Universe is not Locally Real, and the Physics Nobel Prize Winners Proved It" (*Scientific American*, Oct., 2022).

10. References: R. Atkinson, *A New Story of Wholeness: An Experiential Guide for Uniting the Human Family* (Light on Light Press, 2022); C. Darwin [1871], The Descent of Man (current version, CreateSpace Independent Publishing Platform, 2011); D. Loye, *Darwin's Lost Theory: Bridge to a Better World* [updated third edition] (Benjamin Franklin

Press, 2010); K. Johnson, "David Elliott Loye, Pioneer" and E. Laszlo, et. al. "Commentaries on Darwin's Lost Theory: Bridge to a Better World" (in "The Cooperative, Caring, and Moral Nature of Humans: Honoring David Loye," *Interdisciplinary Journal of Partnership Studies* 9(2), 2022).

11. References: K. Johnson, "Evolving Toward Cooperation" (*Kosmos Journal*, winter 2018); D. S. Wilson. *Does Altruism Exist? Culture, Genes and the Welfare of Others*, from Foundational Questions in Science Series, 1. (Yale University Press/Templeton Press, 2015); *This View of Life: Completing the Darwinian Revolution* (Pantheon Books, 2019); D. S. Wilson and E. O. Wilson, "Rethinking the Theoretical Foundation of Sociobiology," (*The Quarterly Review of Biology*, Vol. 82, No. 4, 2007); E. O. Wilson, *The Meaning of Human Existence* (Liveright, 2015), J. A. Agren, *The Gene's Eye View of Evolution* (Oxford University Press, 2021).

12. Based on the Manifesto on Self-governance, drafted by Michael Sandler and Emanuel Kuntzelman for the Laszlo Institute Symposium on the New Paradigm in Politics.

13. Entries are as stated at organizations' websites or in direct correspondence with organizations.

ACKNOWLEDGEMENTS

As presented here, the book in the hands of the reader is the fruit of a heart-warming and exemplary collaboration. The editorial team at Light on Light Press, headed by Dr. Kurt Johnson and Dr. Robert Atkinson, deserves a medal of valour for dedication beyond the call of duty — for heart- and soul-inspired dedication to the cause of publishing a book that conveys a fundamental message in clear and comprehensible language. Ariel Patricia of Sacred Stories Book Publishing and Media also took an active part in this joint venture, supported by Bill Gladstone, the author's long-term friend and agent, Nora Csiszar and other long-standing as well as new-found partners and collaborators. My heartfelt thanks to all of them. They helped me to make this book into an effective channel for transmitting the ideas I have long sought to transmit — and tried to transmit here with more clarity and a sense of greater urgency than ever before.

ABOUT THE AUTHOR

© Photo by Bernard F. Stehle

Ervin Laszlo spent his childhood in Budapest, Hungary. He was a celebrated child prodigy on the piano, with public appearances from the age of nine. Receiving a Grand Prize at the international music competition in Geneva, he was allowed to leave Hungary and begin an international concert career, first in Europe and then in America.

Laszlo received the Sorbonne's highest degree, the Doctorat ès Lettres et Sciences Humaines in 1970. Shifting to the life of a scientist and humanist, he lectured at various U.S. Universities including Yale and Princeton. Following his work on modeling the future evolution of world order at Princeton, he was asked to produce a Report to the Club of Rome, of which he is a member. In the late 70s and early 80s, Laszlo ran global projects at the United Nations Institute for Training and Research at the request of the Secretary-General. In the 1990s, his research led him to the discovery of the Akashic Field.

The author, co-author or editor of 106 different books that have appeared in a total of 25 languages, Ervin Laszlo also has written several hundred papers and articles in scientific journals and popular magazines and is the subject of a PBS Documentary on his life and work. He is a member of numerous scientific bodies, including the International Academy of Science, the World Academy of Arts and Science, the International Academy of Philosophy of Science, and the International Medici Academy. He was elected member of the Hungarian Academy of Science in 2010.

Laszlo is the recipient of various honors and awards, including Honorary PhDs from the United States, Canada, Finland, and Hungary. Laszlo received the Goi Award, the Japan Peace Prize in 2001, and the Assisi Mandir of Peace Prize in 2006, and was nominated for the Nobel Peace Prize in 2004 and 2005.

MESSAGE FROM THE PUBLISHER

Light on Light Press produces enhanced content books spotlighting the sacred ground upon which all religious and wisdom traditions intersect; it aims to stimulate and perpetuate engaged interspiritual and perennial wisdom dialogue for the purpose of assisting the dawning of a unitive consciousness that will inspire compassionate action toward a just and peaceful world.

We are delighted to publish *The Survival Imperative* because this rare book directly addresses humanity's greatest need at this time: raising the level of our individual and collective consciousness to ensure the wellbeing and betterment of the whole. Drawing from a lifetime of distinguished and exemplary thinking from a holistic approach to change and transformation, Ervin Laszlo offers a firm foundation in both history and systems science to make very clear how our current crisis point can be turned around and the critical conditions we face can be resolved. This vitally important book for our time provides much needed insights into the nature of consciousness and where the individual and collective unfoldment of consciousness is leading us. It is not only clear in stating how this will happen but also in providing an achievable vision for taking informed action toward assisting this unfoldment of consciousness.

We consider this book an essential guide with all the needed signposts for navigating our way through the process of global transformation currently spreading across the planet. We are extremely pleased to bring forth this watershed book when the world so needs it.

Managing Editors—

Kurt Johnson, PhD
Robert Atkinson, PhD
Nomi Naeem, MA
Chamatkara (Sandra Simon)

Ingram Content Group UK Ltd.
Milton Keynes UK
UKHW010656250423
420747UK00001B/46